Roger Morgan-Grenville
and Edward Norfolk

The Return of the Grey Partridge

Restoring Nature on the South Downs

PROFILE
EDITIONS

First published in Great Britain in 2024 by
Profile Editions, an imprint of
Profile Books Ltd
29 Cloth Fair
London
EC1A 7JQ

www.profileeditions.com

Copyright © Edward Norfolk and Roger Morgan-Grenville, 2024

10 9 8 7 6 5 4 3 2

Typeset in Sabon by MacGuru Ltd
Printed and bound in Great Britain by Clays Ltd, Elcograf S.p.A.

The moral right of the author has been asserted.

All rights reserved. Without limiting the rights under copyright reserved above, no part of this publication may be reproduced, stored or introduced into a retrieval system, or transmitted, in any form or by any means (electronic, mechanical, photocopying, recording or otherwise), without the prior written permission of both the copyright owner and the publisher of this book.

A CIP catalogue record for this book is available from the British Library.

ISBN 978 1 80081 906 1

Dedicated to the country people of Britain,
who work with nature every day

Contents

List of Tables	vii
List of Illustrations	viii
Foreword by the Duke of Norfolk	x
Prologue: September 2002: A Visit	xx
Part One: THEN	1
1. The Circling Storm	3
2. The Three-Legged Stool	13
3. Beetle Banks and Buzzards	26
4. A Special Delivery	36
5. Forty Years On	45
Part Two: NOW	60
6. Farming for Biodiversity: Early Spring	63
7. Predator Control: Late Spring	76
8. The Scientists: Early Summer	89
9. A Curlew Season: High Summer	101
10. The Soil Underneath: Late Summer	113
11. Dwellers All in Time and Space: Early Autumn	123
12. Lee Farm: Mid-Autumn	137
13. Shoot Day: Autumn	144
Part Three: TOMORROW	158
14. Where Next? A year on	161

Tables	173
Notes	177
Bibliography	183
Acknowledgements	185
Picture Credits	185
Index	186

TABLES
(pages 173–76)

The GWCT wild grey partridge count on the Sussex Downs
Development of grey partridge numbers
Important arable wildflower species recorded 2018–2022
Total insect count at Peppering
Red-listed bird abundance
Development of raptor and owl numbers from 2005–2013

LIST OF ILLUSTRATIONS

Farming system changed from two-crop block farming to multi-crop 'patchwork quilt' approach.
Post-2022, a patchwork of different crops and hedgerows.
Land sharing: a conservation headland for restoring wild arable flowers, with normal arable for food production beyond.
Hedges are laid on a rotational basis to maximise cover at the base.
New hedges are planted on top of newly created beetle banks.
Back after a gap of maybe 50 years, a rough poppy.
From two pairs to a thousand, the grey partridge was always the driver of the renaturing.
A successful conclusion to a clutch reared only feet from a footpath.
The rapid increase in small mammals has seen an equally rapid increase in owls; in this case, the short-eared variety.
A hen harrier flies over the low ground with Arundel Castle in the background.
Bio-abundance in action: linnets and a couple of goldfinch explode from a hedge.
Over 1,000 hares regularly patrol the fields and margins of Peppering.
These days the 'jangling keys' call of the Red-Listed corn bunting is heard throughout the farm.

List of Illustrations

The margins have created a perfect habitat for butterflies; here, a common blue.

Crucial chick food: *Stenotus binotalus*.

Both urban and rural foxes frequent Peppering. Consequently ground-nesting birds need protection through legal predator control.

Predator control is strictly regulated, with humane best practice observed for example, through this Tully trap.

Modern restrainers restrain foxes, which can later be dispatched. The restrainers do not affect badger or deer.

The Red-Listed lapwing has benefited directly from the new management system.

All head-started curlews were ringed; a dozen had GPS attached to them so that their movements could be monitored once they had flown.

Charlie Mellor (foreground) and Graeme Lyons checking insect numbers during high summer.

Driving grey partridges is a highly skilled practice that had to be learned again once shooting re-started.

The shoot is the heart of the team's work. Sometimes numbers will permit only one day a season.

Wild grey partridges star-burst over the hedge as soon as they see a line of guns, making them a highly challenging quarry.

The picking-up team at the end of a successful day.

The Duke of Norfolk (left) and Dr Dick Potts.

FOREWORD

We humans are living on this beautiful planet in an unsustainable way. We are facing unprecedented challenges from global warming. It is a huge problem and we are spending billions annually to try and arrest increased temperatures by cutting carbon emissions. All of this is necessary and we are starting genuinely to wage war against global warming and there are many positive signs we can win. But alongside this we are losing the war to halt nature's decline and it is this which will kill off mankind long before global warming does. This beautiful earth will recover and survive; it is we humans who will not, like the dinosaurs before us.

The tipping point is maybe only twenty years away. There are areas in China and California where natural pollination is already failing. One third of all our food produced globally depends on insect pollination. In China, fruit farmers have tried to pollinate by hand. It's a total failure and to attempt it in Western agricultural practice would cost billions. It would be uneconomic and is simply not a viable proposition. In the United States, large truckloads of pollinators have to be transported to California from Oregon. It is costly and what happens when the pollinators in Oregon run out? The war in Ukraine has shown us that if you take just one cereal-growing area in the world out of production, the effect on global prices is considerable. The whole global food supply chain is much

Foreword

more precarious than we might think. We ignore this at our peril.

Population growth is also presenting challenges and pressures. The global population is estimated at 8.1 billion people and it may peak at 11 billion; no one is sure. But population growth is only a part of the problem. We are all human and each one of us understandably wants a bit more of the world for our families and for ourselves. This is a basic human instinct which is not going to go away. It is wishful thinking to hope otherwise.

All the scientific studies show we are losing nature at an alarming rate. Half of our species are in decline and 15 per cent are Red-Listed – meaning they are in danger of extinction in one generation. Extinction means just that, it means losing a species forever – just like the dodo. We have to take all this seriously. So what is the UK government doing about it? Recently it has set a target that this loss in nature must be halted by 2030 and then there should be a 10 per cent increase again by 2042. This shows a complete lack of urgency, delaying tackling nature's decline for another seven years, and yet the government describes this target as ambitious. It is a pathetic response to a deeply worrying situation. We in Britain have a habit of criticising others throughout the world about their loss of species and habitat. We talk about the shrinking Amazon rainforests, the near extinction of rhinos on the African plains and the vanishing tiger populations in India and Sumatra. Yet the truth is we are by far the worst performer in halting nature's decline among the G10 nations, globally. Recent statistics show this; we have fallen to the bottom of the league. When is the UK government going to wake up and do something about it?

So how are we going to save this beautiful planet from nature's collapse? How are we going to feed ourselves and ensure we have a vibrant economy which can fund all these greening measures and avert the extinction of the species?

The first thing we have to do is all work together to bring about this change. We have to be honest, bury our prejudices and listen to each other. We have to accept the pure truth in science as a whole rather than listening only to the parts we want to hear because they back up our own entrenched positions. We have to come together for the common good of humanity as never before.

Government has to stop dictating from on high with its narrow obsession with procedure. Instead, nature's revival has also to come from the grassroots up, with a focus on outcome, and this will take money, vision and courage. Of course there are many learned scientists who know a lot about their specialist areas and have much to offer in the debate, but so too do the thousands of ordinary working country people who live off the land and witness nature in practice every day. They know just as much and very often more than scientists who focus on their narrow areas of research. If there are existing economic drivers which are successfully preserving nature and biodiversity, and have been doing so for centuries, don't destroy them through ignorance or prejudice or introducing changes for change's sake.

This book explains a twenty-year journey here at Peppering to save the wild grey partridge from local extinction across the South Downs National Park. There is an old countryman's saying: 'The grey partridge is a sign of the health of the countryside. If we have them around, all is well; if we lose them, we do so at our peril.'

Dr Dick Potts, the famous ecologist and environmentalist, had been counting the grey partridge in this part of Sussex since 1966. He probably knew as much about them as anyone else on the globe; it was his life's work. He had witnessed their steady decline. When he walked into my office one day in September 2003 and said, 'Eddie, unless you do something the grey partridge will become extinct locally within five years,' I immediately replied, 'Dick, that's not going to happen on my watch.' These words came out of me instinctively and without hesitation; they came from deep down in my DNA. It was as if there was suddenly a new challenge in my life that I had been born to help with. It was a call to help for a bird I had grown up with from my early childhood, learnt a great deal about and had a great affinity with. Without realising it I had been waiting for this moment all my life and I knew I could help.

My fascination with grey partridges started at my grandparents' home Carlton Towers, near Selby in Yorkshire. From the age of twelve my father and I and my Uncle Michael with his three sons Tom, Dick and Harry used to head up there every 1 September where we walked them up before we headed back to boarding school. A bag of twenty partridges between the six of us was a good day; we used to walk for miles. I shot my first grey partridge with a .410 shotgun on my second day of trying; I can still show you the old oak tree it fell under. The next day I shot another one which towered near the village. The old keeper Bob Foster shouted to my grandfather, 'It's down m'lord vicar's garden, back end.' We stopped everything, went into the vicar's garden and found it. From that moment on I realised how important it was always to respect your quarry and never fail to try and retrieve every bird. I have developed a deep love for the grey partridge ever since.

I must mention here my father because even though he didn't really like shooting, he loved any excuse to head up to Carlton for a family party. He was a loving, charming and very brave man.

After the collapse of France in May 1940 while serving as a

The Return of the Grey Partridge

captain in the Grenadier Guards he found himself at Dunkirk. When I was at Oxford, a corporal who had served under my father at that time came up to me and said, 'You don't know me, but I owe your father everything.' He explained that in the retreat to Dunkirk he was shot in both legs, unable to walk and abandoned by a hedge for the Germans to pick him up as they advanced. My father said to his corporal, 'I'm not leaving you here, I will be back.' My father walked for several miles, found a wheelbarrow in an old barn, and then came back to collect the corporal and wheeled him the whole way to the beaches at Dunkirk. He got off back to England and avoided five years in a POW camp or worse. This was typical of my father.

My father didn't talk much about the war until the last year of his life which I think was normal for that generation. Their experiences were too horrific to dwell on, they just buried them and got on with life. The truth was Dunkirk was a hell on earth: constant bombing by stukas and the RAF nowhere to be seen. They felt completely abandoned for those six days. Everyone was at the limit of human endurance with no food, hardly any water and completely exhausted by the constant bombing and fear and lack of sleep.

The Royal Navy was present in great force, but the destroyers couldn't get within half a mile of the beaches because of the shallow sea. What changed everything was the flotilla of small boats which arrived from all along the south coast of England and then ferried the troops out to the destroyers as well as back to England. This spontaneous civilian bravery was truly extraordinary and as a result 343,000 Allied troops escaped back to Britain against the Navy's forecast to Churchill a week earlier of 10,000–15,000 troops maximum. They had to leave all their equipment behind on the beaches, but Britain still had an army. We were not yet beaten.

Foreword

My father became friendly with a French officer of the same rank and they both made sure all their men were off the beaches before they finally queued up on the Mole (a long and wide breakwater) themselves and boarded a Royal Navy destroyer on the fifth day. When they walked over the gangplank they were greeted by an able seaman with two pints of beer and two copies of the *London Evening Standard*. The French officer turned to my father and said, 'Miles, any nation who can do this at a time of such chaos and adversity – you will never lose this war.' He was, of course, right. That summer Britain stood alone in Europe and kept the flame of freedom alive long enough for America to join the war; the rest is history.

My father got his M.C. three years later in the push through Italy. He was Brigade Major when the British advance came to a complete standstill near the River Sangro. His Military Cross citation read:

> The leading troops were held up in a very exposed position and subjected to sniping, shell and mortar fire. At all times Major Howard's coolness, cheerfulness and above all his infectious enthusiasm for the battle were an encouragement and example to all who came into contact with him. When the tanks were held up by mines and the operation was halted, Major Howard undertook several recces on foot and showed the greatest energy and coolness in complete disregard for the enemy fire, spreading cheer and optimism wherever he went.

During the war there were two ways of being awarded a Military Cross. Most were given after being mentioned in despatches and endless debate followed for months about who was worthy of what. The other way was to be granted it immediately for outstanding bravery. My father's was the latter signed by General Alexander of Tunis G.O.C. of 1st Army Group. It read simply, 'Immediate M.C. – Alexander.'

Behind the positive façade my father always struggled with a degree of diffidence. But on that cold November day in Italy in 1943 he achieved something which he was immensely proud of all his life, and yet he hardly ever talked about it.

So why am I telling you all this? It's simply to remind you that previous generations have had their own problems to solve, their dark days where survival and victory seemed like a distant dream, but they didn't give up hope. They found the courage, vision and humility to come together as a nation and succeed. That is what we have to do today to avert nature's collapse and the food shortages, chaos and anarchy that will surely follow and threaten the very survival of mankind.

The Peppering grey partridge project is by no means unique in offering a solution to reversing nature's decline. It is just one possible solution among many, which happens to be working. It offers a middle way for arable England, with 85 per cent of the land still producing the food we need through modern regenerative farming, and just 15 per cent dedicated to nature's revival. It has an economic driver which makes it sustainable for the long term and the shooting does not cost the taxpayer one penny. Partridge numbers have recovered from near extinction in 2003 to about 1,000 grey partridges or more annually every year since. And on the back of this many red-listed species of birds, wild flowers and insects have recovered to levels not seen since the 1930s. It is one the most successful nature revival projects of its kind in Europe, and it is talked about as far away as South Africa as a beacon of hope.

The main driver is a day's partridge shooting which can be let for a very significant sum, valuable income that allows us to persevere with our environmental projects and keep our biodiversity recovery project alive. A team of guns arriving at Peppering will not sleep very much the night before. At breakfast there will be a buzz in the air because everything shot that day will be entirely wild. It will be a shooting experience of a lifetime, a step back in time. Standing 30 yards behind a tallish hedge, waiting for a covey of greys to suddenly appear, twisting and turning and star bursting over them. A right and left will be treasured in the memory and the skill required by the many beaters and flankers behind the hedge is also considerable. Despite all best efforts, about a third of the partridges will outwit man and go back over the beaters' heads, and no amount of flag-waving will deter them. The old cock and hen partridge seem to be able to remember exactly what happened the year before and they will have none of it.

The other main part of the pleasure on a day's shooting at Peppering is the birdsong. The skylarks, finches, linnets, corn buntings, yellowhammers and the birds of prey which remind one of an old England treasured in the mind but rarely seen today. And the 120 different types of arable wild flowers in the conservation headlands with 600 different species of insect which depend on them, still glowing in the autumn sun. The sheer wonder of it all and the realisation that given half a chance nature can bounce back and there is still time to reverse its decline. None of this is rocket science but it is attention to detail in a professional, focused way, with legal and sustainable predator control carried out by a team of dedicated keepers from February to July each year. In this way a rebalance of nature is carried out during the nesting season only, which gives all threatened ground-nesting birds a chance. In July all traps are removed, and nature is left to take its course again for the rest of the year.

The Return of the Grey Partridge

I firmly believe that if we all act together we can achieve great things. There is still time to restore Britain to the top place in the nature revival league. That is where we should be, that is our rightful place. Government has to lead from the front on this. It needs to rewrite our targets to be far more ambitious to bring about a revival in nature now, and not wait until 2030, by which time it may all be too late. The land management practices involved on a wild grey partridge manor are some of England's best kept secrets, as this book explains. DEFRA, Natural England, the RSPB and other local nature reserves must take note of what can be achieved. This is a wake-up call to charitable and publicly funded nature reserves to start trying to match the results in the private sector, particularly bearing in mind the millions of pounds they consume annually.

My plea to government is for a more constructive and efficient relationship with the private sector to work with us and allow us to flourish in nature's revival by working together. Don't hold the many thousands of country people of England back. Instead ask: how can we help? Value what we already have and allow Britain to play its rightful part again in nature's revival before it's too late.

Edward Norfolk

Foreword

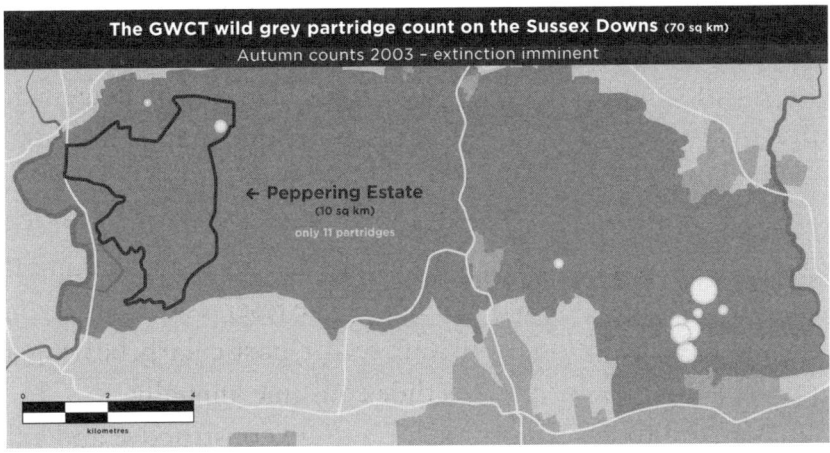

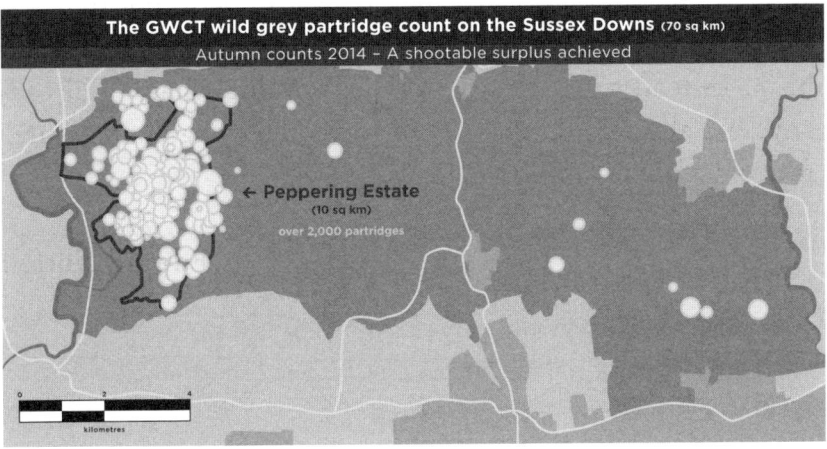

◯ circles signify a covey of partridges

PROLOGUE

SEPTEMBER 2002: A VISIT

Absences creep up on us, unheeded.

Like a slight lowering of the evening temperature, we often notice them only when we have to reach for the extra layer of warmth, or when someone brings them to our attention. We generally register all the things we see and hear, but not those that have receded into the half-light or have simply disappeared for ever.

It is only when a physical change highlights what has gone – a view opened up by a missing tree, for example, or the contrasting shades of a wooden floor from which an old rug has been removed – that something within us is triggered. It may start with the simple sense of there being something amiss, and the journey from that point to the understanding of loss is a long and complicated one.

But inevitably one day we come to understand the simple truth that something we once had is no longer there for us, and we are gradually diminished by this and by the slow aggregation of all the other losses in the course of a long life.

Whether local or complete, they are personal extinctions, and they matter.

All extinctions matter.

Dick Potts generally started his autumn stubble-counts on the first Monday of September, when there was still warmth in the

September 2002: A Visit

air and the sun slanted low across the Downs, throwing long shadows across the fields. That's when the grey partridges were easiest to count, out there in the first light among the ruts and furrows near the margins of the great fields, and he had been doing his stubble-counts for more than three decades.

Anyone observant, and up with the lark, might have seen him in his green Subaru before the first stripes of light had filtered across the eastern sky, making his slow way up the Peppering hill from Burpham onto the South Downs that morning in 2002. It was a journey that he had been making at this time of year for the last thirty-seven years, since the outset of what he called his 'Sussex Project'. This was an initiative to better understand what lay behind the long-term decline of the grey partridge, and to create and communicate appropriate management techniques that could then be shared with the farmers on whose land he worked. He loved this place and felt instinctively at home among the soft folds, high fields and long, dry valleys where the Downs dip down to meet the River Arun, the mists from which rise up to meet the trees. Apart from anything, it was perfect grey partridge ground, and grey partridges were what he had dedicated most of his long professional life to. If anyone in England was qualified to do this work, it was Dick Potts.

Everyone on the Peppering Estate knew who he was, even if they couldn't say what he was doing. They knew Julie Ewald too, who had come over from the flatlands of the American Midwest in 1995 to do expert mapping analysis with Dick, collect pesticide data and decipher his appalling handwriting. They were also familiar with many of the rest of their team who came each year and collated two weeks' worth of intensive data from the six farms contained in the study area. Their routine was to do a dawn count of the grey partridges and a

The Return of the Grey Partridge

dusk count, and they would fill the hours in between with the myriad different ecological observations and recordings of the land that Dick felt privileged to be a part of. In his pack and his car he had everything he needed to complete this new chapter of his long-running survey, and normally he troubled no one. From these intense periods of research and observation would slowly emerge the moving timeline of the health of the biodiversity on the chalky South Downs.

As an ecologist, he lived in hope, but he also saw earlier than others the trends that were heading inexorably, and increasingly steeply, downwards. On this particular Monday in 2002, by the time they had finished their dawn count, Dick knew without question that he had to go down the road and share the news of what he had just seen.

'Do we simply keep on monitoring them into an inevitable local extinction?' he asked Julie rhetorically, as he packed his binoculars back into their case. 'Or do we try to do something?' He told her that he would be back directly.

Their project was already fighting to keep even a reduced share of its original funding, and there wasn't going to be much point in returning each year to mark down the word 'zero'. You could do that from the office in Fordingbridge, without driving a single mile.

So he climbed into his car and headed back down the hill, along by the water meadows at Wepham and up to the offices of the Norfolk Estate.

Eddie Norfolk was sitting in his office, drinking coffee and trying hard not to notice a headline in the copy of *The Times* on his desk that annoyed him. After a while he turned it over to the back page and got on with his work.

He knew that Dick Potts was around and, having only ever

September 2002: A Visit

met him briefly once before, had left a message for him to drop by, if he happened to call in at the estate office. It was a busy day and, with routine work spread out over his desk, he had more or less forgotten about the invitation when there was a knock on the office door and Peter Knight, the estate manager, came in.

'Dick Potts is downstairs at the moment if you want to see him.'

A few minutes later, a robust-looking man in his early sixties walked in. In some ways, he looked as if he had come off a safari: pale chinos with a faded pink shirt and a loose birder's waistcoat, open at the front. His skin had the healthy sheen of a man who spent a very large percentage of his life outside.

'Morning, your grace,' he began, in a Yorkshire accent that had been softened a little by years of living in the south.

'Call me Eddie, please. It's a huge pleasure to see you. I keep hearing so much about what you are doing up here. How's it going?'

There was a pause, during which Dick ordered his words as carefully as he could.

'It's a pleasure seeing you too,' he said. He shifted his weight a bit. 'But I've just been up at Peppering, doing the count, and it's all a bit of a disaster. Even more of a disaster than before.' He seemed to be taking it all personally, as well you might if you had spent half a lifetime with the bird whose local extinction you were about to foreshadow. He looked shattered.

'Tell me,' said Eddie.

'Five pairs. That's all we've got left up there, I'm afraid. Eleven birds. If nothing can be done, there won't be a single bird on the western end of the Downs within a couple of years. Ten at the outside.' Dick was simultaneously charming and desperate. What might, for the wider world, have been a little

xxiii

local extinction of a bird that most people never saw anyway was nothing short of a catastrophe for a man who had dedicated well over half his working life to their cause. And not just anywhere; but right here on the Downs. Also, as a highly accomplished ecologist, Dick knew all too well that, as for the partridge, so for all ground-nesting birds. The fate of the much-studied grey partridge spoke eloquently for the silence of the others.

As a boy, a few decades earlier and a couple of hundred miles north, Eddie had been brought up with those 'greys'. He had known them, and worked with them, since he was eight or nine. He had learned all about them, walked them up and shot them. From the age of fifteen, when his grandfather died, he had been in charge of the keeper, who was, in turn, in charge of the greys. Eddie knew their natural history like the back of his hand: how they laid the biggest egg clutches of any bird on Earth, how they scuttled invisibly along the hedgerows until they burst into the sky on rapid wings that curved down like those of a red grouse and flew so rapidly over the contours, as if to the element born.

'Five pairs?' Eddie repeated quietly, as if calibrating the new information. 'That's all we've got left? Five pairs.' He didn't wait for an answer. 'Well, we won't let them go, Dick. Not on my watch.'

Once there had been thousands of greys up on the hill, but the last century had enveloped them in an almost perfect ecological storm. It was not unreasonable that the hedgerows had been torn out and the fields expanded to make vast prairies, as that was what the government had told all landowners to do, to pave the way for giant cereal fields after the near-starvation of the Second World War. It was not unexpected that the wild seeds and insects that form the partridge's diet had disappeared

September 2002: A Visit

under a constant battering of pesticides and herbicides, as the seeds came from weeds that were no longer welcome in the new way that farming was being undertaken. And it was hardly surprising that the predators had increased at the same rate as the partridges had decreased, since the old structure of the keepers who controlled them had died in the Flanders trenches nearly a century before or never returned to work.

Eddie knew instinctively that Dick was right. Deep down, he had probably known it already for years anyway. And as for the grey partridge, so for the skylark, yellowhammer, corn bunting and lapwing. And as for the ground-nesting birds, then so for all the hares, field mice and dung beetles out there. *Perdix perdix* may well have been just one species but, in the chalkland habitat up on the hill, it spoke for a hundred more, and then another hundred after that. 'When we try to pick out anything by itself,' wrote the early conservationist John Muir, 'we find it hitched to everything else in the universe.'

This wasn't so much the death of a single bird as the crumbling of an entire ecosystem.

It was one thing to say, 'Not on my watch,' but quite another to set the wheels in motion to make that a reality. Apart from anything, the 800 or so hectares on which Dick based the work that he did, and which would therefore have to be changed beyond all recognition to alter things for the partridge, weren't even Eddie's to change. Two of the farms were out of the estate's control on three-generational tenancies, while the third, Home Farm, had let out its shooting rights for the next twenty years.

So while Dick climbed into his car for the journey back to work on the hill in a rather more cheerful state than he had anticipated thirty minutes earlier, Eddie looked out of the window for a time and thought it all through. And then, after

The Return of the Grey Partridge

a few minutes, and with the coffee now cold on his desk, he walked down the stairs to the estate manager's office.

'Peter,' he said, 'I've got an idea.'

This is the story of how the fulfilment of that idea, alongside the many people who worked on it, led directly to one of the most quietly successful recent renaturing projects in Europe.

It is the story of the return of 'the grey'.

PART ONE
Then

1

THE CIRCLING STORM

Everything must change for everything to remain the same.
Giuseppe Tomasi di Lampedusa, The Leopard

Where do stories start? In nature, what is a beginning?

Is it the bacterial gatherings in the vents of the ocean depths, from which we all came? Or is it, for the grey partridge, the evolutionary moment 200 million years ago when pterosaurs went from being an awkward flier of short bursts to master of the primeval skies? Or, 20 million years ago, when one of the species that started to evolve away from the African francolin developed into a partridge? Or later, when a descendant of that bird found it too cold on the rising Tibetan plateau and drifted its way downwards, and westwards, towards Europe? Who knows? Evolution is an eternal process, not an event, and we are merely observers in a fraction of a slice of our planet's time. If the timeline of the Earth was a twenty-four-hour clock, the age of human written history would be a mere tenth of a second.

We have to start somewhere, so let it be 450,000 years ago in a small community of *Homo heidelbergensis* near the present site of the Sussex village of Boxgrove. There, among the detritus of rhinoceroses, bears and voles are the bones of grey partridges and the first sign we have that they have been

The Return of the Grey Partridge

among us since the dawn of what we know as time. Like us, after that they came and went, normally southwards, and normally at the behest of the periodic freezes brought about by moving glaciation, but it is clear that they have been part of our lives since then. Far more so than the red-legged partridge,[1] the fossils of greys have been found all over Europe, in 700 layers and 246 separate sites.

That Boxgrove bird was probably very similar to the grey partridge that we know today. For all we know, it lived a life of plenty. After all, back in the Pleistocene era (the last Ice Age), apex predators such as lions, wolves and spotted hyenas would probably have kept in check the partridge's middle-rank or mesopredators, such as the fox or the stoat.[2] And, after all, humans hadn't yet become the Anthropocene adaptor of environments that has marked their ascent-at-any-price for the last 10,000 years. Meanwhile the grey partridge continued to adapt to a particular treeless terrain, nesting on the ground, eating seeds and developing the ability to survive cold winters. Unlike many of the other 11,000 or so bird species, the partridge didn't feel the need to become migratory; on the occasions it did, it tended simply to be field by field, rather than hemisphere by hemisphere. If the ecology is suitable where you are, not being migratory removes a good deal of risk from a species, as most songbirds might confirm. Even now, a dispersed covey of grey partridges seldom goes much further than a half-mile from where it started.

Partridges have been important to man for longer than you might think. There is evidence, mainly from France and Spain, that he has been hunting them for more than a quarter of a million years, cooking them for at least half that time and actually rearing them for the pot for a few millennia.

Meanwhile the subspecies of the wider partridge family

evolved by separation caused by different lengths of glaciation, and by the comings and goings of large bodies of water. It is thought, for example, that the African chukar[3] split from the European red-legged partridge by the rapid filling of the Mediterranean Sea.[4] Over the millennia, around forty-five separate species of partridge have evolved, now covering a broad range of Europe, Asia and parts of North Africa. It is also worth noting at this early stage that, however similar the grey and red-legged partridges may look, they are in fact very different birds, connected only as recently as 20 million years back, somewhere in Africa, and from something that probably looked much like a modern-day francolin. The first red-legged partridge didn't in fact set foot on British soil until King Charles II brought some over to Windsor Great Park from the Loire Valley in the 1660s, itself about 400 years after Henry III had once had 2,100 greys served up for his Christmas lunch.

Shining a spotlight onto our more recent history, we find that the grey partridge would have lived alongside its fellow grassland species in the hedgerows and stubble fields of old England. Until the agricultural revolution (about 300 years ago), even though greys would have been shot perched on the ground, or netted, or hunted with hawks, the effect on their numbers would probably have been minimal. If the advent of organised shooting – or 'shooting flying', as it was first known – started to reduce the numbers of game birds, particularly as the technology and skill behind shotguns accelerated, then the practice of rearing birds artificially more than reversed it. Ever since then, one of the unsolvable mysteries of game management has been the stark impossibility of rearing grey partridges that will go on to fly naturally. Rear them artificially and they will just gather in enormous flocks and move as one, providing all the sport in one short moment.

But, all things considered, the breed was a highly successful one, familiar throughout its Sussex territories until a twenty-year-old Bosnian Serb happened to fire two shots into the bodies of a middle-aged couple sitting in a stalled Gräf & Stift limousine in a Sarajevo street on 28 June 1914.

That altered everything.

There is almost no upper limit to the cultural change that the subsequent carnage in the Great War trenches brought about.

From the country houses and estates of Britain flocked butlers, chauffeurs, gardeners and valets to answer the call that Lord Kitchener shouted down from every poster on every street corner of the land. But it was from the fields, hedgerows and coverts that the gamekeepers went in their thousands, and largely never came back. In 1914 there had been 23,000 of them; by 1918 this had been reduced to less than half;[5] killed, shot, maimed, gassed or traumatised, those who came back to the same jobs as before were a fraction of those that had gone out. Sandringham alone lost nine keepers, and three of the four who had gone from the Wentworth Estate in Yorkshire made the ultimate sacrifice.[6] The imposition of death duties by the post-war government meant that many estates were simply no longer viable, and many of those who had survived the war and had gone back to work found there was no work to return to. And the first effect this had, back home, was the proliferation of predators on those estates. In this instance man is the apex predator and, freed from the vigilant keeper, the mesopredators underneath, such as stoats, crows and foxes, multiplied. And as they multiplied, so the game on the ground suffered and diminished.

More was to come on 1 September 1939.

When Germany invaded Poland and set in train the Second World War, Britain was about to receive a very sharp lesson in quite how self-sufficient it wasn't in the matter of its food production. With U-boats intercepting the ships carrying anything from Canadian wheat to Jamaican sugar and African pineapples, the island nation came as close to starvation as it ever had. On the eve of hostilities, the country was importing just over 20 million tonnes of food each year, including half its meat, 70 per cent of its cheese and sugar, 80 per cent of its fruit and 70 per cent of its cereals.[7] During the war the government took direct control of the nation's farming, and its War Agricultural Executive Committee instigated a huge wheat-growing programme that rapidly led to the ploughing up of grasslands and the pulling out of hedgerows. The effects were extraordinary, including the addition of 10,000 square miles to food production, and the country's dependence on imports halved.[8]

Once the war was over, a silent battle continued on the land between the farmers – mainly small ones, who wanted to see a return to a grassland system – and the National Farmers' Union, which pushed hard for greater subsidies that would lead directly to greater wheat production and, from that, to larger fields. The subsequent decline in the little family mixed farms tells you more eloquently than I can who won the argument.

By 1947 subsidies had been fully introduced, and in subsequent years there were grants for grubbing out hedges, ploughing up hillsides, removing meadows, pulling out orchards and draining vast tracts of land, up to 100,000 hectares a year at its peak.[9] Given that half of all species decline is down to habitat loss, and 80 per cent of that loss is down to agriculture itself,[10] there is almost no overstating the grim effect this policy had on any biodiversity that wasn't directly related to feeding human beings. The countryside, which had looked remarkably unchanged for centuries, suddenly took on the aspect of a prairie land, with huge fields hosting cereal monocrops, with the inevitable decline of the ground-nesting birds this foreshadowed. Above Arundel, the only certainty was that the fields on North Stoke and Peppering farms were getting bigger and bigger, sweeping from ridge line to ridge line until the wildlife-rich hedgerows had been more or less eradicated from memory. A walker on the forerunning tracks of the South Downs Way[11] at the time could be forgiven for thinking they were in Alberta and not near Arundel.

While this new settlement was in progress, the development of increasingly capable and powerful machinery was cutting the need for manpower. Most of the people were absorbed into new roles in the burgeoning service economy, but the effect on the wider rural culture was enormous: with fewer and fewer people involved on the land, or reliant upon it for their living, there were fewer people to care about it and to notice when things within it were changing and declining. A highly urbanised population tends not to worry too much about the disappearance of a particular songbird or a huge decline in butterflies, and the education system certainly didn't encourage people to worry themselves about the part these things played in the local ecology, or would come to play in their own lives once they had disappeared. Politicians wanted the old mixed rotational farm dead and buried, and largely they got their way.

Other factors were coming into play at the same time, almost all of them detrimental to good stewardship. While the old tenancy agreements had been predicated on the maintenance and improvement of the land, the new subsidy regime simply promoted yield at any cost, and it was difficult to blame or criticise farmers for merely doing what the government was begging them to do. Indeed, it would have been very difficult for most of them to have made any sort of a living unless they toed the line.

The accession of Britain into the EEC (forerunner of the EU), with a Common Agricultural Policy that defied common sense as much as it wrecked biodiversity, simply made the problem worse. In all, since 1945 there has been a 65 per cent decline in the number of farms, a 77 per cent decline in farm labour and a fourfold increase in yield through the effects of intensification.[12] And more recently, the growth of intensively reared game bird shoots, particularly pheasants, has attracted increased numbers of predators like a magnet, which, finding the pheasants protected by the wire netting of a pen, swiftly turn their attentions to more accessible prey.[13]

Thus, as the Great War had largely done for sustained predator control, so its successor did for the grey partridge's habitat. All that was needed now was to see which way Harold Wilson's 'white heat of technology' would push things during the last third of the twentieth century. The answer, if you were a hungry grey partridge chick with a healthy appetite for insects, was not an encouraging one.

There is evidence that chemicals of some sort have been used to control pests and diseases for more than 4,000 years,[14] but it was not until the commercial release of the herbicide 2,4-D in 1946 that their use became routine on farms in the industrial West. Dick Potts reckoned it was the 1975 first use of a crop-spraying plane on his Sussex Study area that set the immediate course for a 31 per cent decline in bug life on those farms, particularly as he already knew Rachel Carson's research demonstrating that poisons accumulate incrementally within bodies as they go up the food chain.[15] By the 1980s, chemical compounds such as demeton-S-methyl and cypermethrin were being used liberally on farms to control new threats such as orange-blossom midges; in the case of the latter, Potts calculated that it took a full seven years for the sawfly (a bug that hurts nothing, but feeds partridges) to recover its population after just one application.

But Dick was already an old hand at this by the time he was a teenager and was miles ahead of most of his peers. As a boy on the farm in Yorkshire, he had once asked a shepherd why he always drank so much milk during the working day. 'It's the only way', the shepherd had told him, 'that I can protect myself from this sheep dip.' Later on, as a PhD student on the Faroe Islands, Dick had noticed the softness of many of the cormorants' eggs and had been able to trace it back to the DDT run-off in their fishing grounds. He was twenty-five when Rachel Carson's *Silent Spring* was published and, from then on, he was in the vanguard of those who made a lifetime's work of trying to yank farming back onto a course that didn't lead directly to destruction. Years later, his wife Olga articulated this as his mantra: 'Give nature a chance, and nature will always come through.'

None of this damage was intentional or even foreseen, but still it accelerated. By the 1990s the assault on wildlife, which was already having to cope with a general unnatural tidiness that had anchored itself within modern farming, now witnessed a whole bunch of new pesticides. These included the new neonicotinoids, which didn't even need to damage a food source in order to damage a partridge; they could do it directly. Season after season, new treatments were tried on the crops in those huge new fields, from the first treated seed to the last pre-harvest pesticide, and season by season the land suffered. Twenty-one insecticides alone were used on the Sussex Study area between 1970 and 2000, with the effect that even the ecologists couldn't work out which ones were doing the most damage. But then, in a country where the population of the grey partridge had declined by around 90 per cent in fifty years – from more than a million to well under 100,000 – there were probably more important priorities.

Perhaps nothing sums up the situation better than the temporary local extinction of the Knotgrass Beetle, a favourite food of the grey partridge, which even inspired its own lament at the 2001 Proms. Ironically, on the issue of climate change, Potts was neutral about its effect on the grey partridge, tending towards being slightly positive, on the basis that a decent percentage of the birds' insect diet was actually benefiting from the rising temperatures. These days that view has to be seen against the contrasting one, which is that warm weather (above 20°C) during incubation reportedly reduces rates of productivity by up to 70 per cent, and wet Junes (another apparent by-product of climate change) drastically undermine chick survival. Underneath it all, though, Dick understood that the inexorable rise of the global human population, which had jumped from 3.5 billion to 6.4 billion in the first thirty-five years of the Sussex Study (and has jumped to 8 billion since then), would mean that the pressure on the quiet margins of farmland would go on being relentless.

And it's not as if these problems, and these declines, were limited to the Sussex Study area, or to the grey partridge. Not by any means; not then, and not now. If you took an average worldwide result of man's baleful efforts across 4,000 tracked vertebrate species, you would be looking at a 68 per cent decline between 1970 and 2016, or 94 per cent if you had the misfortune to be in the American tropics.[16] And where birdlife is concerned, the ground-nesting birds of the South Downs take their place alongside 3,967 bird species that are on the way down in the rest of the world.[17] It turned out that the same human beings who had mastered the secrets of synthetic biology to precision-engineer their own species couldn't even keep a simple partridge alive.

Dick Potts used to describe the conditions needed for a thriving population of grey partridges as a 'three-legged stool' involving the right habitat, abundant food and effective predator control. Remove any leg of the stool, he said, and the rest of it would slowly collapse. He knew many things as he drove back down that road from Peppering to Arundel that September morning in 2002, but the urgency in his voice was brought about by knowing that not just one, but all three, of the stool legs had collapsed.

To save the grey partridge – even if it was possible – would mean changing an entire ecosystem.

2

THE THREE-LEGGED STOOL

If you want to make small changes, change the way you do things; if you want to make big changes, change the way you see things.
Gabe Brown, American regenerative farmer

Nature works at its best when it is allowed to function in some sort of equilibrium. The tragedy of recent biodiversity loss is that this has rarely been allowed to happen.

On the face of it, the situation for any ground-nesting bird in an island full of predators, and with variable weather, would seem precarious. However, over the centuries and the millennia, checks and balances start to exert themselves, so long as man is not involved. If a prey population crashes after a hard winter, for example, the associated predator numbers will come down as well, which will, when conditions improve, allow for a relatively swift revival of fortunes for both. If a local disaster – say, a flood – causes a local population to reduce or kills it off altogether, then surrounding groups that were unaffected by the flood will start to seep into the untenanted territories in the months after the waters recede. For millions of years species have slowly risen and fallen at the behest of the natural rhythms of the Earth, its weather and according to their relative fitness to survive in the prevailing conditions.

The Return of the Grey Partridge

Ironically, for all the catastrophic declines we have inflicted on our planet's biodiversity, our own de-natured species finds it easier to empathise with the prey animal than with the predator. The squeals of a rabbit being killed by a stoat trigger in us some primal support for the underdog, a regretful shaking of the head at the cruelty of nature. We may well mourn the loss of a chaffinch from our bird table to a sparrowhawk, but we would do well to remember that the latter is outnumbered by the former by a factor of nearly ten to one and is declining rather quicker.[1] The problem is not the sparrowhawk.

No, the problem is us. It arises from the age-old habit of that apex predator of all apex predators – man – to wish to adapt the world around us to our own needs, rather than to tailor the way we live to the holistic needs of the planet that we occupy. This behaviour has given rise to the unofficial term 'Anthropocene', both as a description of the age in which we find ourselves and as an adjective to accompany the sixth extinction period that, tragically, we are supervising. When our hunter-gatherer forebears first domesticated animals 10,000 or so years ago and so became agrarian, there were probably around a million of them on Earth, their numbers always restricted by the need to be on the move and therefore to wait until children were mobile too, and only then breed again. Today that number has multiplied by a factor of nearly 8,000, and extinctions are running around a hundred times faster than they would without human impact. What 'Anthropocene' ultimately means is that we will be the first animal (and presumably the last) to change the geology of the planet, let alone anything else.

To understand the wider context of what had been happening at Peppering with the grey partridges, we only have to start by holding up a mirror. The demands that our appetites and needs are collectively putting on the thin crust of soil that wraps some of our planet, its oceans and its biodiversity are truly astounding, and the grey partridge is just one grain of sand on the beach of collateral damage. It joins a number of other birds, such as goldfinch, lapwing and song thrush, as an indicator species for the health of our farmland biodiversity, fulfilling the conditions of being representative, reactive to environmental conditions and responsive to change in a predictable way.[2] If the grey partridge is fine, then the land probably is as well; if it isn't, the opposite applies.

So having led the grey partridge into this mess, it is only we who can lead it back out again. Ironically, using the primary principle of first aid – that of removing the patient from the source of danger – this was actually rather more straightforward than you might think.

It was the birds' great fortune that enough people at Peppering understood this from the start.

Peter Knight, for one. He well understood the approaching challenge.

He had come down from his native Cotswolds in the early 1980s to take over responsibility for the estate's farming operations and had been the overall estate manager since 1989. A countryman by birth, and with a countryman's instincts at heart, he had instinctively known of the gathering Armageddon for ground-nesting birds like the grey and needed no persuasion to want to reverse it. Often he had found himself walking on the hill with Dick Potts during his visits, chatting about the cost of farming's modern methods and of the seeming impossibility of running profitable farming and active conservation alongside each other. What Peter was now being asked to do was to come up with a farming system that could restore biodiversity that would work alongside, rather than against, food production – in other words, a 'middle way'. And with only three pairs of grey partridge on the land, he knew that he was in a race against time before they became locally extinct. Indeed, it was only a few weeks before one of the few remaining birds from Dick's study area was killed by a walker's dog, leaving just two breeding pairs.

It was not as if there weren't examples elsewhere of targeted efforts to bring nature back into, and alongside, the farming process. Up at Raveningham in Suffolk, keeper Jake Fiennes had gained permission from the landowner in the late 1990s to take the least productive 20 per cent of the farm out of food production altogether and had quickly seen extraordinary gains in biodiversity in consequence. 'On the land set aside for nature,' he later wrote, 'we used no fertiliser, no fungicides and no pesticides. The absence and shortage of wild game birds was reversed. After a few years, we had hundreds of grey partridge.'[3]

Others were looking at the same approach. But in many ways, much of the approach was to be no more complicated than looking at each farming decision and simply assessing it against its likely future environmental impact. Grey partridges hadn't failed because they were in some way a fragile species; they had failed because everything they needed to maintain and increase an active population – open ground within easy reach of protective cover, for example – had been removed from them by the way in which the place was farmed.

'It has to start', Peter muttered to himself as the Duke left his office, 'with us actually controlling the three farms.' Two of these were in long-term agricultural tenancies, while the third, Home Farm, was leased to another branch of the family. He took a large piece of white paper and laid it on one side of his desk, determined to write down each thing that needed to be done as it came into his head.

The Three-Legged Stool

1 Take North Stoke and Peppering farms back in hand

The first of these was easier than the second, as the tenant farmer had already passively indicated that he might be amenable to giving up the farm. Besides, the dairy there had closed down, contractors were doing most of the work, and diversification was replacing agriculture as the focus of activity. Proving once again the value of a policy of maintaining good relationships with all the estate's stakeholders, Peter raised the subject and soon went up to North Stoke Farm to thrash out a deal. Three months later the farm was back in hand. Peppering Farm took a little longer but, by 2006, it too was back.

In Peter's office the piece of A3 paper was slowly being populated with what needed to be done. Dick Potts had been quite clear from the start that shooting – or rather the prospect of it sometime in the future – would have to be the incentive that drove the partridges' recovery. Although it might seem counter-intuitive that the best way to rescue a species was in fact to plan to shoot any excess, it was entirely logical from the land-management point of view, in that what was good for the partridge was good for just about everything else. Dick agreed with the Duke that 90 per cent of the land would be used for farming, as before, with the remainder given over to conservation measures that could then attract some compensating money from the range of stewardship schemes that the government was offering. While the new mathematics might never again quite add up to the previous profit, they could get there or thereabouts, or so it was felt. Within the long conservation debate between land-sparing (setting aside large areas of land for rewilding and free from agriculture, as a means of increasing biodiversity) and land-sharing (making food production and biodiversity projects work alongside each other), this one came firmly down on the latter side. Onto the paper went the next task.

2 Radically reduce the average size of each field

Reducing the size of the fields meant, of course, dividing them up, but to do so with bird and insect habitat uppermost in mind, which meant keeping them in a state of permanent vegetation. For some years an accepted way of achieving this had been to create 'beetle banks', which were little more than raised strips of earth running through the middle of the field, generally two metres wide and under half a metre high, which were then sown with grasses and tall-growing wild flowers, thus creating a localised haven for insects.

Farm workers who, until recently, had been taking part in the normal activities of modern arable agriculture suddenly found themselves being briefed to spend their days running directional ploughs up and down the middle of a field, both ways, forcing ridges to emerge that flew in the face of intensive farming. Over the coming years fifteen miles of these banks were constructed over the various farms, and most now lie at the base of large conservation hedges. By the time they had finished, the number of fields had grown from thirty-eight to ninety-three, while their average size had come down by nearly two-thirds, to eight hectares. Prairie had gone back to patchwork quilt.

3 Create strip cover alongside all existing and new hedgerows

A few metres of plant cover that was tall enough to provide cover, yet short enough to be accessible for food, had for some time been a solution for partridge management. It enabled the birds that nested in the hedgerows to hunt for food without becoming a target for raptors as soon as they left the hedge. Partly by reading scientific papers and partly by simple observation, the team soon realised that, like humans, the birds had likes and dislikes in the insects they ate: large rather than small, for example; green and yellow over brown and black, and almost never red. A diet of caterpillar, sawfly and beetle larvae ticked all the boxes, which was obviously good news for ladybirds and in turn started to dictate what should be planted in the cover strips.

However, from the very start Peter knew that at least one thing was firmly on their side: the fact that, in terms of egg-laying, the grey partridge is one of the most productive birds on Earth. If they could get everything else right, the chances were that the greys could breed themselves back into a healthy population much more quickly than, say, if they were dealing with single-egg seabirds. Eighteen eggs in one clutch was normal, and even twenty-five was not unknown. In a really good year, with a dry June and other conditions aligned, a pair of greys can routinely end up with around eight or nine fledged chicks.

The general fertility promised sunlit uplands, but just about everything had to change first.

Andrew Stringer, who had been the previous tenant's keeper at North Stoke for more than a decade, was quite surprised to get a call while he was away in Yorkshire celebrating his fiftieth birthday. He wasn't a big one for communication at the best of times, and certainly not when he was on holiday, but he recognised the dialling code and took the call. He knew Peter Knight well and had recently found out that the Norfolk Estate was taking North Stoke back in hand.

'Sorry to disturb you, Andrew,' said Peter. 'But any chance you could come in to the estate office when you get back and meet up with the Duke?'

Andrew didn't need to be a clairvoyant to know what the

meeting would probably be about, but not which way it would go. Also, the interest they had shown in him was puzzling. He was a reared-pheasant man, and not a wild-partridge one. If anyone in his family understood the greys, it was not him, but his wife, Heather, who had reared them under broody hens when she was a girl in the 1960s, when a mysterious man used to bring them up from Littlehampton. Andrew found it hard to believe that he had much expertise to offer, concerning what was, in effect, a wild shoot.

As a boy, he had learned his craft alongside his uncle, who would take him ferreting among the farmland hedgerows and pigeon-shooting in the copses that dotted the countryside. He had come down to Arundel from his native Hertfordshire a decade before, to help set up and run simulated game-shooting for the previous owner, David Locke, in the wake of the catastrophic forestry damage of the 1987 and 1990 hurricanes. And while the clay-shooting days had worked well, it wasn't long before he was persuading David Locke that the damage to the woods was more superficial than first thought and that it was entirely feasible to get the pheasant shoot going again.

Over the subsequent years the unorthodox little shoot had gone well, with a few simulated days alternating with high pheasants off the steep wooded banks, and then flighted duck down on the low ground by the railway line. It paid for itself, and the success had not gone unnoticed by the neighbours. All the same, Andrew wasn't sure that he wanted much change in his life, at the age of fifty.

'When I went to Peter's office,' he told me twenty years later, 'I wasn't quite sure if I'd have either a job or a house at the end of the meeting.' But as the conversation went on, he started to understand the depth of passion the Duke seemed to have instilled, not only in Peter, but in everyone else on the close-knit estate, especially among the farming team who were, after all, going to have to implement most of the changes that would be needed. Equally, Andrew could see that what they were really talking about was really no more than a change in the way they farmed the place – easy to overcomplicate. He found the Duke roaming the corridors after he had finished the meeting with an acceptance of the offer.

'Did you accept?' the Duke asked.

Andrew replied that he had.

'In that case, have as many days as you want on the pheasants, with my pleasure. Just get rid of them.'

Not every keeper got asked by his boss to shoot as much game as possible in as short a time as he could; it wasn't exactly what keepers did. But in the hierarchy of game-bird feeding, the pheasant was a very muscular competitor with the smaller grey, which was going to need all the help it could get.

It was a sign of quite how much things were going to change at North Stoke.

In many ways, Dick Potts had long ago laid down the blueprint for what needed to happen, for the remainder of what got written down on Peter's large white sheet of paper.

The beetle banks would all be planted with hedgerows towards the end of the winter, for a start, and perennial weeds would be choked back by undersowing grass into the wheat and barley. As the fields became smaller and more numerous, so there would emerge a patchwork quilt of crops, and a rotation that at once maximised the yields and provided a safe and reliable food source for the grey partridges. The key was to avoid one crop being alongside the same one in a neighbouring field. And that, the management team kept reminding themselves, was the whole point: this was not going to be some exercise

The Return of the Grey Partridge

in artificially rewilding a block of land for the sole purposes of shooting and biodiversity, so much as proving that profitable farming could feasibly take place alongside the wholesale renaturing of the land.

To the surprise of some, Eddie made it clear from the start that 90 per cent[4] of the land would still be farmed commercially, not even organically, and that a creative tension would therefore need to exist between the farming and sporting teams, with him refereeing, if matters ever reached an impasse. Sometimes this would be simple, like the complete ban on harvesting during the hours of darkness, so as to avoid mowing down young coveys; but at times it was much more nuanced, as the management of nature tends to be. It was in the edges and headlands (traditionally the area at each end of a field where the machinery is turned around) that the difference would be made; where once the wheat and barley had extended, prairie-like, from hedge to hedge across the vast fields, from now on there would be ten-metre conservation headlands around each field between the strip cover and the crop, full of clover, cornflower, sow thistle, yellow chardock and bastard cabbage, and other perennials that would provide food for the invertebrates that would, in turn, do the same for the partridges.

And still the list on Peter's paper grew. Overwinter stubbles would be reintroduced, and fencing laid down on either side of the many footpaths to keep the walkers' dogs away from both the livestock and the nesting partridges. In the hope that partridge numbers would quickly grow, grain feeders were situated at 100 metre intervals along the new beetle banks, so as to reduce the amount of time the birds spent making themselves vulnerable while feeding out in the fields. At the same time and for the same reason, supplies of small-sized grit would be provided around the place; grit, an essential element for the

The Three-Legged Stool

processing of the seed diet in the birds' gizzards, was plentiful around the estate, but mainly in open places where the birds would be targets for raptors as they searched it out.

And there was more. There would be no further releasing of other game birds for shooting – not only to keep the chances of disease to a minimum, but also not to distract the keepers from the core of their work. So much so that Eddie would often half-joke that the quickest way to leave his employment in a hurry would be to secretly rear just one game bird rather than letting it rear itself. This prevented, at a stroke, a suite of tried-and-tested ways of getting the birds back onto the land, such as releasing autumn coveys, rearing eggs under bantams and then securing adoption by barren pairs or just getting the grey to rear its chicks in the security of captivity. From the very start, the sport side of the vision set out that every grey partridge on the ground had to be utterly wild. And not only every grey partridge, but every other bird as well.

No grey partridges would be shot until there was agreed to be a shootable surplus – that is, an excess of birds above the available land's ability to carry them.[5] And even when there was, if the surplus wasn't felt to be sufficient, the team were (and still are) prepared to miss out an entire season in order to maintain the health of the population. But in spite of all the planning, the work and the investment, it was to be eight long years before a single shot was fired at a grey partridge; moreover, on two occasions since that day in 2009, the entire season has been cancelled, so as better to preserve the stock. Even though shooting has been the driver and enabler of the project from the start, it has always been subservient to the prevailing situation and the conditions on the ground.

Ahead of almost all this in importance was to be a step change in the legal control of predators that would go hand in hand with the other measures. A ground-nesting bird in the south of England faces many predators, and always has. When there are healthy populations, it is no more than in the nature of things to lose a few along the way to a sparrowhawk, say, or to a stoat or a fox; no more than an equilibrium that has been acted out in nature since the dawn of time. But when their numbers are already down to single figures, and there is a queue to eat what remains of them that includes weasels, rats and crows, not to mention all the protected raptors, then something has to change. Indeed, nest-cams have recently shown that it is not just the 'traditional' predators that can cause damage; under the cover of darkness roe deer and sheep have broken the eggs for their calcium; and even the odd spiteful wild cock pheasant has kicked the eggs away and then walked blithely on.

Ironically, one of the relentless predators of ground-nesting birds are dogs that have been allowed to walk off their leads during the breeding season, meaning that (equally ironically) one of the most significant expenses has come in the form of providing robust fencing to provide protection in the hedges from the four-footed users of the footpaths – a problem that could be solved better by the owners simply putting animals on a lead in the spring and early summer. The target species for the predator control, though, were strictly the ones permitted by the regulations – specifically fox, stoat, weasel, rat and corvid – and the main control would be done between January, when the breeding cycle was beginning, and early August, when the chicks were big enough to start making their own way in the world.

Thus were painstakingly set in place the three legs of the stool required for the project: a suitable habitat, an abundant food source and a legal measure of protection from some of the main predators. Peter Knight's sheet of A3 was nearly complete.

He had one of the three farms, which was a start, and he had a beat keeper he respected and with whom he could work.

But even as the landscape was being transformed, one thing remained painfully clear: with only two pairs of grey partridges, the population – such as it was – was on a knife edge. One bitingly cold week a lucky raptor, or a couple of uncontrolled dogs, was all that would be needed for a local extinction. It was simply too much to expect the renaissance to stem from just four birds.

3

BEETLE BANKS AND BUZZARDS

In preparing for battle, I have always found that plans are useless, but planning is indispensable.
General Dwight D. Eisenhower, 34th President of the United States, 1953–61

In the dying days of 2002, aside from farm machinery and the bark of an occasional dog fox, the huge fields of Peppering were largely silent.

Back in 1914 a gamekeeper leaving his cottage in the early morning might have seen huge flocks of lapwing above the ploughed fields, heard yellowhammers, corn buntings and cirl buntings singing in the hedgerows and noted hundreds of turtle doves arriving from their migrations; he would surely have seen stone curlew up on the hills, heard the 'wet-my-lips' call of the quail and, if he was lucky, heard the grating 'crex crex' of the corncrake. Grey partridges would have vastly outnumbered the red-legged ones, and hares were everywhere. But let's not imagine too rosy a picture, for that same keeper would have seen to it that the place was almost devoid of raptors. Sparrow-hawks, buzzards, goshawks and peregrines had been persecuted into a sullen absence, with maybe the occasional marsh harrier venturing in from her nest down by the water meadows at Burpham. In all probability, the only near-raptor that would have been seen with any regularity was the little red-backed shrike, and only then because it was far too small to bother the game birds.[1]

In 2002, where once there would have been those huge flocks of lapwings, the furrows were now bare of nests. Scrub breeders like nightingales, whitethroats and yellow wagtails had vanished, as there was no longer enough scrub to breed in. Finches, too, had declined through the ongoing lack of overwinter food and a lack of spring breeding opportunities, as had the thrushes. With so few birds to feed on, the raptor numbers had collapsed too. The only birds that thrived on the land were opportunist crows and rooks, adaptable seagulls and lucky old pigeons, for which the abundance of grain had brought unexpected riches. Such birdlife as there was generally announced itself in shades of grey, black and white, and with a raucous caw.

Apart from the crop that was being grown, the fields were largely empty as well. Seventy years of maximising yields through the efficiencies of vast fields, ploughed to their very edges, had reduced the mixture of wild flowers to a shadow of their former variety. The wheat and barley carried their seeds too high to be of any use to the ground-nesting birds, while most of the arable weeds had been sprayed away by whatever was the chemical of choice the previous spring.

Small wonder the partridges had gone.

Nick Field had other things on his mind than grey partridges.

Already the tenant of Splash Farm, a small dairy operation between the villages of Wepham and Burpham, he had bid successfully for all the arable contract farming work on what had, until recently, been a large dairy unit at the estate's Home Farm. At the age of thirty-three, this had brought him an entirely

The Return of the Grey Partridge

different level of responsibility and opportunity to what he was used to, starting with the need to invest in the machinery that he would need to do the job properly. He answered directly to Peter, and knew of Dick Potts only as a regular visitor waving cheerfully from some hedgerow or other.

Having said that, he knew something was up, long before Peter came down to his farmyard one January morning. When a tenanted farm is taken back in hand on an estate such as this, it is big news among the locals and hard to keep quiet.

'Do you know what a beetle bank is?' Peter asked.

Originally conceived as places in which predatory insects and spiders could overwinter in the artificial boundaries within large fields, beetle banks are constructed so as to allow the beetles to move quickly out into the crops as spring arrives and thus keep some natural control over the pests. Their long, grassy mounds can also act as barriers to run-off and soil erosion when laid across slopes and, as a side-benefit, provide habitat for ground-nesting birds, small mammals, amphibians and reptiles, particularly when a gap is left between the end of the bank and the boundary of the field, thus breaking a predator's logical journey in. In the relative emptiness of a large arable field, a beetle bank can also act as a little pulse of biodiversity, not to mention as an insect larder.

Nick knew only a little about beetle banks, which were quite a specialist development of the last few years, and told Peter so.

'I need you to go and create a couple up at the top of North Stoke. I'll go up there with you and explain, so that we get it right first time.'

They bumped up the chalky track in Peter's Land Rover and parked up by Canada Barn, a largely derelict set of buildings high up on the ridge that looked down the Arun Valley to the sea.

'These are going to be banks with a difference,' Peter said as they walked down together through the heavily ploughed land. 'As soon as you've done them, we're going to put hedges in.' He explained that the hedges would serve multiple purposes, as far as future grey partridges were concerned, in that they would both give some protection against the attention of sharp-eyed raptors and provide natural lifting points for some future day when the birds would be driven towards a line of guns.

The technique was simple, if time-consuming, starting with the striking of a line down the middle of the field, and then ploughing inwards from about six metres on either side of the bank, until the earth in the middle rose up. The process needed multiple passes this way and that, but eventually the long mound in the middle would rise up to somewhere between half and two-thirds of a metre high, and there would be a shallow depression on either side, where the soil had been. The key was to make a bank that was slightly higher than the one you needed in the long term.

Because this would leave a relatively unstable bank with a natural tendency to slide gradually back into the dip again, grass would first need to be sown, and quickly. This, in turn, needed some ancient and modern ingenuity: modern, in terms of the harrow that Nick rigged up to the back of his old quad-bike to create a decent tilth along the bank; and ancient, in the form of an old seed fiddle,[2] with which Peter walked up and down, broadcasting the seed, as if in a long bygone era. Finally, Nick hitched a little roller to the back of the quad-bike and rolled the grass seed in. If you were looking for self-help conservation, you would have needed to look no further than the creation of the first two banks. Then again, if you were looking for a major revolution in the way things got done, this was a particularly gentle one.

At first Dick Potts was not at all convinced about the hedges, suggesting that it was a waste of effort and money, but Eddie was insistent that they were required from the start. Dick's recent background was at the Game & Wildlife Conservation Trust, which had first come up with the idea of beetle banks during the 1990s, and whose research didn't suggest that hedges were a necessary addition. Gradually, though, as he saw how many ground-nesting birds – greys included – chose the hedges to nest in, and how many of the local raptors were now flying fruitlessly above them, he relented, realising that a nesting grey on a marginally covered bank was a sitting target for just about any of them. Two decades later there is not one metre of beetle bank across the whole 800 hectares that doesn't have hedging above it. Indeed, as this book was going to press, the last of a total of 185,000 hedging plants were being planted in the chalk of some newly acquired ground, so as to create almost twenty miles of new hedging.

The hedges that went in were a traditional mix of mainly hawthorn, but also blackthorn, hazel, field maple and spindle, and then holly (for the year-round foliage) and guelder rose (for its flowers). By this time more banks were going up around the rest of North Stoke – work that would eventually include Peppering and Home Farm. By the time the various farms had been brought together and the job done, there would be fully fifteen miles of new hedgerows planted, consisting of well over a quarter of a million plants.

The landscape was changing quickly, and the irony was not lost on some of the older estate workers that many of these new hedgerows were simply replacing the ones that the government had insisted were grubbed up in the aftermath of the war, some in roughly the same alignment as they had been previously, and others in completely new places. While this was indeed true, it didn't devalue the project at all, which was merely setting out to prove, among other things, that the passing of the old mixed-farming model of agriculture had come at a terrible cost to biodiversity. To this day, Peter insists that all he was doing was pushing the clock back half a century on the edges of the fields, at the same time as driving up yields and earnings from the middle. This was no reinvention of the wheel.

Few of the thousands of walkers who passed by on the footpaths each year would have realised at the time the magnitude of what was going on. For sure, even the least observant might have noticed the signs of hedge-planting and bank creation, but it would have taken a certain knowledge of the workings of the land to see that, while the fields were getting smaller, a patchwork quilt of crops was replacing the vast open prairies of wheat and barley that had been there before. Wheat and barley were still an important part of the farm's production, but to these were added oilseed rape, peas and other legumes, depending on the market.

From Nick Field's point of view, it all meant more work and longer journeys. Whereas previously he could have been drilling all day in one large field of, say, winter barley, from now on he would have to do so in three or four different places, each normally at the opposite end of the estate from the last. But then that had been the deal from the very beginning: the wildlife and the farming had to go hand in hand, so that at least 85 per cent of the income of the farm could be sustained while every metric of biodiversity improved. He had known that when he signed up, so he wasn't going to start complaining about it now.

In those early days the entire grey partridge team in the North Stoke Farm pilot area consisted only of Eddie Norfolk, Dick Potts, Peter Knight, Andrew Stringer and Nick Field, and it was to be several years before other experts and agencies were to get involved. It was the five of them who planned and executed the new manner of farming, walking the tightrope between what was good for the ground-nesting birds and still being profitable for the farming operation. If there was an alchemy afoot, it was simply the coming-together of the Duke's passion and eye for detail, Dick's encyclopaedic knowledge of the grey partridge, Peter's wide-ranging knowledge of farming and land management, Andrew's practical understanding of what made a game bird tick, and Nick's ability to convert their knowledge into changes on the ground.

As the man responsible for the bottom line of the farm, Peter knew from the outset that the extra funding available from the various national and European Union schemes would be essential to the viability of the whole project. With a bit of luck, it might just about cover the revenue that would be lost from the lower yields.

'With twenty different Higher Level Stewardship and Countryside Stewardship schemes available across the estate, it was not a programme for the faint-hearted,' Peter says in hindsight. He had to laboriously pick out which was the best scheme for which piece of ground, then make all the sums add up for the entire estate. 'Given that at least 10 per cent of the estate's arable land is under Natural England schemes, it probably took up to a quarter of my time at certain stages of the year.'

This was further complicated by the many options within each of the schemes, such as undersowing, beetle banks and wild-bird mix, all of which had to be evaluated before the support was applied for. A surprisingly large part of the long-term success of the project probably comes down to the relationship that was built with Natural England from day one, including the fact that successive project managers at the agency saw this as a venture that ticked just about every environmental box within their remit. Natural England was, and is, the gatekeeper to the financial schemes that enable projects like this to happen.

From all this early work emerged a few basic principles that were felt essential to the long-term success of the project. First, whatever was done had to be seen to represent good value for the taxpayer, who was, after all, largely subsidising it. So when, for example, the first new dewpond was dug after a few years, it was deliberately sited *near* a public footpath, rather than secreted away on some private part of the estate; this, in turn, enabled the walkers to benefit immediately from the extraordinary upswelling of nature around the ponds.

Second, the estate should miss no opportunity for PR. Large private estates tend to be, almost by definition, secluded and almost secretive places, unless they are deliberately setting out to be public; at Peppering it was quickly realised that the long-term success of the project needed the active support of its wider stakeholders. This could be as simple as telling the beat keeper to abandon the old gamekeeper's habit of stringing his vermin kills along prominent fence lines, or as subtle as putting up signage that helped to inform passers-by what they were looking at.

The third, and possibly most important, principle was the understanding, built into all decision-making, that what was good for the grey partridge would also be good for the vast majority of wildlife. While it was obvious that other ground-nesting birds would benefit from what was being done, it was less so (at least initially) that this would also provide better conditions for every other bird group, as well as for small mammals and insects. Perhaps no species has benefited more than the hare; once a rarity, it is now head keeper Charlie

Mellor's view that there are more than a thousand of them packed into the 800 hectares. Looking down on the fields with a night-vision scope these days, where the bulk and shape of the hare gives it a very obvious heat-signature, one sees that they are alive with jills doing the rounds of the furrows to suckle their concealed leverets.

Ironically, an increase in raptor numbers has been widely welcomed, as the numbers tend to be a visible airborne reflection of the health of what is going on in the ground below; it was the rival game birds from neighbouring shoots that became the problem. From the diseases and parasites that many reared birds carry – which can cause devastation to the small population of grey partridges – to the habits that both pheasants and red-legged partridges have of 'dropping' their own eggs into the formerly camouflaged nests of the greys, and bullying behaviour at the feeders, they are almost always bad news. Add to that the reared pheasant's unwitting habit of attracting a host of new predators into the area, predators that will then happily kill a partridge if they come across it, and a strange situation emerged in which pheasants that people were paying good money to shoot three-quarters of a mile away were being shot as vermin all through January at Peppering.

Meanwhile, Peter and the Duke became increasingly convinced of a fourth principle: that there needed to be a robust scientific basis behind the decisions that were being taken. While the three-legged-stool metaphor provided a good basis for general actions, which really consisted just of reversing decades of damaging land management, it was important that everything they did conformed with current best practice. Thus an invitation went westwards to Dick Potts in Fordingbridge, asking him to become the consultant ecologist; and with speed and enthusiasm, the invitation was accepted. From then on, until health and age started to prevent him from doing so, Dick was the estate's consultant ecologist, botanist, ornithologist, lepidopterist and entomologist, all rolled into one. But then if you wanted only one '-ologist', Dick was probably the one you would have chosen.

Thus it was that, in the summer and autumn of 2003, the new landscape slowly took shape, with banks and tiny new hedges demarcating the new field boundaries, and the patchwork quilt of rotational cropping becoming an agricultural reality. Slowly but surely, the missing elements of biodiversity were already seeping back into the grasses, hedges, ponds and fields: a corn bunting seen like an echo of the past on a fence post; a dung beetle alongside some roe-deer droppings; or a rough poppy emerging bravely out of the late-summer stubble. Equally, they could provide all the habitat and food in the world but, with only a small handful of grey partridges, the risk of a local extinction was still a pressing and real one. The idea that there might one day be enough to have some sort of shootable surplus was still like a lantern out on some distant moor.

As it turned out, 170 miles to the north-east, Dick Potts happened to have a particularly helpful friend.

4

A SPECIAL DELIVERY

Every new beginning comes from some other beginning's end.

Seneca

David Clark ate his supper early on the night of 3 March 2004.

Night work was in no way unusual to the Sandringham head keeper, although what he was being asked to do this particular evening was not among what he would think of as his normal list of jobs. Two days earlier he had been approached by his employer, the Duke of Edinburgh, and asked if he had enough grey partridges to spare a few pairs for the Arundel Estate.

'I'd like to send them five if I can,' Prince Philip had said. 'But only if you tell me that we can afford to lose them.' He then added that he knew there had been huge habitat improvements made in Arundel and he felt the greys would have a good chance of surviving, and then going on to breed.

Sitting opposite David at the kitchen table in his cottage that evening, clasping a large mug of tea, was Dick Potts. They knew each other well and, were it not for decorum, the request could easily have come direct from one to the other, instead of between the bosses. Not only did they know each other but, because they had worked together on the Arundel Partridge Survival Project many years before, David knew intimately the

A Special Delivery

ground that his birds would fetch up on and was instinctively keen to help it happen. Indeed, it was there that he and Dick had once seen what was the biggest fledged covey – a pair and twenty chicks – that either had ever come across.

Putting on their boots, coats and hats against the crisp March night, both noticed the slight evening breeze getting up. They went to the yard where nine of the estate's beat keepers were waiting for their briefing and explained the plan.

Over the years, the Sandringham grey partridges had leaked out from the beats where they had been raised and were now settled in most parts of the estate. Greys always fly into the middle of the field to roost for the evening, so as not to leave a scent trail, and the plan was therefore for each beat keeper to take one of his own fields and simply observe where the birds had flown to. Once it was fully dark, and with the aid of a night-vision scope, they could drive almost alongside the resting pair and simply net them on the ground, then place them in a basket. Often it didn't end up being as easy as this, and David had crafted various ruses, such as playing the recording of a familiar tractor from the front of a Land Rover, to create the illusion of it being a normal farming evening.

Late on in the evening, David remembers one of his beat keepers, Roy Norman, netting a pair and then accidentally losing the cock into the shadows of the night. 'God alone knows how he did it,' he recalls, 'but half an hour later Roy emerged out of the darkness on his quad-bike with the cock bird in a basket on his lap. That was an amazing bit of keepering.'

Shortly before midnight their combined efforts had captured nine pairs – considerably more than either Duke had asked for or offered. However, Dick was keen to start with as many as possible, and David wasn't going to quibble over the extra four. One by one, they placed each pair into its individual collapsible cardboard crate, designed for carrying poultry, which had been sourced from the Warburton vet the day before by the Arundel head keeper's wife. If royal treatment would help these Sandringham birds into their new lives at Arundel, then royal treatment they would get, no matter how many people were involved in providing it.

So it was that, as the Norfolk keepers headed off to their various cottages to sleep, Dick Potts climbed into his car, then turned left on the A149 to begin his long drive through the night to his charges' new home.

It was still too dark to confirm for himself that it was Dick's green Subaru, when Andrew Stringer saw the headlights of the car that was bumping up the track from North Stoke towards him the following morning, 4 March. Then again, if it wasn't Dick, any self-respecting beat keeper would want to know who the hell it was on his patch at that time of the morning.

He had woken at 2.30 a.m., an hour before his alarm was set to go off. Although he only had to drive about a mile up the track into the Downs from his cottage, and his breakfast could wait until the job was done, Andrew knew instinctively that this was probably the most important day of the latest part of his career and did not care to risk being late. For the previous twelve months the team had been working full time to create an environment that would give these new arrivals the best possible chance of survival. Indeed, what had enabled the Duke of Edinburgh and his head keeper to send those birds down to Arundel in the first place had been the knowledge of the extensive lengths that had been gone to in order to achieve this. Beetle banks, hedges, headlands, margins and the patchwork quilt of rotational farming were by now showing themselves physically on the ground. Granted, the hedges were still small, but the ground beneath them was alive with food for the arriving partridges. Andrew's job had been mainly to start taking a grip on those predators that he could legally control, which had been increasing in number for the last three decades.

The day before, he and Dick had sited ten foot by thirty foot wooden pens – one for each pair of greys, and a few to spare – dotted around the new hedges on the beetle banks below Canada Barn, coincidentally the first ever bank they had constructed. When he ascertained that it was, indeed, Dick's car, Andrew greeted him with a flask of tea and then helped carry each of the nine pairs in their boxes towards their allotted pens. He held each bird steady as Dick applied the red leg-rings that would enable them to identify them in future as Sandringham birds.

By the time the first traces of light were making themselves apparent in the eastern skies they were done, leaving Dick to head off to bed after what had been a full twenty-four hours awake, and Andrew to wonder what would happen next.

In the event, what happened next was surprisingly little, on the surface at least.

Each morning and evening in the coming weeks after the greys' release from the pens, Andrew went out with his binoculars and holed up along the adjoining hedgerows to see whether the new birds were still there, which they were, with the exception of one pair that was never seen again. In view of the fact that they found no bodies or feathers, the collective view was that the pair had simply slid down the side of the hill into a neighbouring patch of ground and a suitable bit of farmland. With regard to all the others, the greys were not only regularly spotted around the place, but stayed paired and all soon produced clutches of eggs, which alleviated instantly the fear that they wouldn't settle and would avoid breeding.

The Return of the Grey Partridge

In his report six months later, Dick was able to point out that there were now no fewer than eighty-eight grey partridges on the North Stoke ground – 'already ten times the national average' for that area. Although the data on insects had not yet begun to be collected, he noted that the recovery of other ground-nesting birds and rare arable plants had been no less amazing; and 44 per cent of all sightings had been of those red-ringed Sandringham birds, which, in his view, now made up more than half of all the grey partridges on the estate. He forecast that, if none were shot, the eighty-eight birds could be expected to produce no fewer than twenty-five pairs the following spring, as against one for the same season two years earlier. Ironically, he added, the biggest threat to the new population that he could foresee was being killed on one of the adjacent shoots. After all, someone swinging a gun at a small, fast-moving bird that has just burst over the hedge line in front is unlikely to have time to discriminate between Red-legged partridges and greys.

Dick came to the conclusion that success over the coming winter depended, at least in part, on improving the number and dispersion of feeders. These, he said, should be removed from the wooded areas that were still dominated by pheasants, and placed in the beetle banks and, because these hedges were new and still quite sparse, placed under the cover of *Cupressus* wigwams to protect the birds from the attention of harriers and sparrowhawks. The feeders didn't only help the partridge population; over the season Dick had observed feeders also being used by chaffinches, bramblings, woodpigeons, stock doves, pheasants and rooks, and he felt that each month would disclose even more. He also noted that a flock of sixty of so linnets seemed to have made its home on the new set-aside, and that the density of skylarks had doubled to about thirty pairs per square kilometre (0.386 square miles). With barn owls back, and with whitethroats, starlings and finches all on the increase, the general birdlife was increasing with a vibrancy that even Dick hadn't expected. In fact, from all these sightings, and from the return of hen harriers, goshawks, peregrines and hares, he calculated that numbers were now roughly similar to what they had been back in his Sussex Project 1971 census. In other words, just eighteen months' work had reversed three decades of decline.

It was the same story with plants.[1] In a nine-day period in June 2004 Dick and two experts found no fewer than eighteen new species in natural regeneration set-aside, including thyme-leaved sandwort, spear thistle, chickweed and the all-important knotgrass. To general delight, they were also able to identify Venus's looking-glass, prickly poppy, bladder campion and narrow-fruited cornsalad, all of which had been absent for as long as any of the locals could remember. Dick was far too experienced an ecologist to be surprised by the power of nature to bounce back, but even he was taken aback by the almost unbelievable speed with which it was doing so.

He ended the report with an opinion that, although the time was still some years away, it was no longer beyond imagination that Eddie would one day soon have a shootable surplus of grey partridges back at North Stoke.

A few months later he wrote personally to the Duke of Edinburgh, beginning: 'Sir, I feel sure that you would like to hear more good news. The excellent results that I reported on 31 July became even better as the last of the harvest was cleared: one Sandringham pair had a wonderful brood of seventeen.' He was able to finish by politely declining the Duke's offer of a second consignment in the spring of 2005. 'Like Eddie Norfolk and the rest of the team, I feel we really have enough birds, especially if they do as well as last season.'

It was not a way in which Dick had expected to be able to sign off.

Twelve months on and there was still general amazement at the greys' fecundity.

With the hedges growing higher and, even more importantly, thicker, the September census in 2005 had raised the number of greys on North Stoke from eighty-eight to 212, a ninefold increase since the project had been launched in 2003. The success of the project led to the idea of trying to get Peppering Farm and Home Farm back in hand as well, to give the project a greater area.

Dick's report proudly contains a graph announcing that the last two years had been the best successive ones since 1976, when the ultra-dry summer produced the best conditions for partridges for decades. The increased number of feeders had done their trick, although it annoyed him to see that they had also attracted unhelpful numbers of pheasants, whose schoolyard-bully appearance at the feeders would tend to scare away anything smaller. Dick had done a good deal of work over the Channel on the shoots of northern France and was generally at pains to point out, to whoever would listen, that one of the reasons the partridge numbers were so strong over there was that they usually didn't have to put up with pheasants. The accompanying maps in the report confirmed that pairs of greys had distributed themselves widely all around the farm's new hedgerows.

If the grey partridge numbers had been surprising, the increase in other birds was little less than astonishing. Ground-nesters like the corn bunting, yellowhammer and skylark, which were generally affected by the same issues as partridges, were thriving; linnets had gone from being locally extinct in 2003 to being just about the most numerous bird in the area two years later. And the faster the numbers of songbirds increased, the faster the raptors increased alongside them, especially the hawks, for which they would be prey to be taken on the wing. This in turn meant that a more limited number of grey partridges would be killed by raptors, which represented a return to equilibrium. No conscientious landowner or gamekeeper minded sharing the game with these magnificent hunters when there was more than enough to go around.

The team was learning lessons all the time. Close-planted kale strips, they found, contained such a high concentration of weeds that it became almost impossible for a partridge chick to move through them when it was wet, whereas – to widespread irritation – the birds seemed to thrive down in the neighbour's oilseed rape; creeping thistles had to be removed and burned as soon as they were cut. Above all, the policy of patchwork-quilt farming that was entering its third year provided for different crops on each side of the hedge, which required different crops at different times of year.

An incidental mark of quite what those nine pairs of greys had started came a few years later, when Peppering found itself in the position to return the compliment, or at least pass it on, and send pairs of their own birds to other places in Sussex, Wiltshire and Hampshire that were starting on the same journey. A letter to Eddie in March 2010 from a nearby estate that was keen to follow in their footsteps acknowledged receipt of five pairs that had recently been sent over, and gave an upbeat progress report, exactly as Dick had done to the Duke of Edinburgh six years before.

'Hopefully, the weather will stay warm and give us a better spring than last year in terms of food for the chicks,' the letter finished, 'and I will let you know how the pairs and their offspring progress.' It is a remarkable feature of the early stages of rescuing a species from local extinction quite how important the welfare of individual birds and their partners is.

As a foretaste of where the grey partridge project was inexorably headed, Dick noted as the final point of his report summary in October 2005: 'To the wider world perhaps the most important benefit may be the near incredible resurgence of the cereal ecosystem flora. Kevin Walker [the DEFRA consultant overseeing the botany of the agri-environment measures] now considers North Stoke to be a botanical site of National Importance.'

The N and the I were in capitals, and everyone understood why.

5

FORTY YEARS ON

What is called genius is the abundance of life and health.
Henry David Thoreau

By the start of 2006 the local grey partridge population was thriving to such an extent that the small size and eccentric shape of North Stoke were unable to hold it, and the excess birds were leaking off into neighbouring territories, including Peppering, a larger farm to the south-east.

On a purely human level, it was irritating to lose birds that had taken so much hard work and expense to bring to their thriving state. On the one hand, it was simply nature in action, a subtle relocation of territories to follow the rapid growth in population. On the other hand, it was almost certain to lead the displaced coveys into immediate, and possibly terminal, trouble. Dick Potts had carried out post-mortems on fifty-one grey partridges at North Stoke to see what was still killing them and had observed at least ten causes of death,[1] most of which would only be enhanced in the open and more intensively farmed neighbouring ground. Nearly two-thirds of the birds had fallen prey to sparrowhawks and hen harriers, which was acceptable natural wastage near the protective hedgerows and margins of North Stoke, no more than the equilibrium between a healthy mix of predator and prey. But transpose that to the open fields of Peppering and it would soon become a relentless hunting-down of each covey until it was gone. It wasn't just that the birds would be lost to North Stoke; it was that they would soon be lost altogether.

It is the estate manager's job to be well informed, locally at least, and Peter Knight had been aware for some time that the family who held the three-generation tenancy of the 445-hectare Peppering Farm was perhaps losing its long-term interest in the operation. As had been the case at North Stoke, it looked as if the land was going to be farmed by outside contract, an outcome that would simply bake-in the intensive prairie-style agriculture and make any potential for influence less and less likely. To ask a tenant farmer to surrender an agreement is a tall order, but with a willing seller, and with the price of grain at its lowest level for years, it was achieved without drama. The Duke carried out the negotiation with the tenant farmer, Toby Collyer, himself and shook hands on the deal one Sunday afternoon in December 2006. And the fact of Peppering coming back linked the hitherto-split farms of North Stoke and Home Farm, so the latter was duly brought into the mix as well.

This time Nick Field knew in advance what he would be asked to do (more beetle banks) and when (very early spring), so he ensured that he was ready. Once again Eddie, Andrew and Peter stomped around the area deciding where to place the hedges, always being guided more by the potential flight of the birds than by the historical delineations. When they were done, Peter briefed Nick, and Nick simply got on with it. Thus were the huge fields subdivided by banks, and thus were the banks planted up with hawthorn-dominated hedgerows as soon as possible. The additional work was absorbed by the team with no significant extra expenditure on manpower, and the ethos of concentrating on good, well-motivated staff guided by minimal management continued.

*

While Dick Potts's 'three-legged stool' analogy created the direction of travel for work on the ground, the absorption of Peppering back into the project came as a stark reminder to everyone involved that the costs and numbers created a pressure all of their own. It was one thing being sustainable as far as nature was concerned, but quite another being sustainable financially. To create a haven for wildlife in general, and grey partridges in particular, on the relatively small expanse of North Stoke was something that could just about be financed privately, almost as a means of proving concept; but to do so on a full 800 hectares of commercial farmland needed some very detailed engagement with the various support schemes involved.

From the start, Eddie and Peter agreed that the subsidies and grants would be expected to make up only what was lost through the reduced acreage of intensive farm activity, which meant that all the costs related to the shooting – keepers, housing, quad-bikes and much else besides – would have to come from income generated exclusively by the shooting. This made things much easier and more realistic, when planning and negotiating with Natural England.[2] It was the immense good fortune of the project that Peppering's gatekeepers at Natural England saw the point and were supportive from the very start, and that continuity was assured by the fact that there were only two of them in the first fifteen years. Other estates tell a very different story.

The early work was done between Peter Knight and Alex MacDonald from Natural England, and mainly consisted of deciding which areas would be covered by Entry Level Stewardship and which by the more generous Higher Level Stewardship, and then which of a suite of subsidiary options should be added. The resulting scheme enabled capital grants to be given towards the increasingly expensive activity of creating around ten miles of new hedging (on top of ten miles of new beetle banks), which, in turn, meant that the farm wasn't committed to increasing its borrowings to make it happen. Capital support was also provided for the construction of a network of fencing between some of the footpaths and the wild-flower mixes that led to the nesting sites, partly for livestock and partly because a small proportion of walkers believed, and continue to believe, that the right to exercise dogs off the lead during the breeding season trumps the right of ground-nesting birds not to be eaten while sitting on their nests.

'Oh, he's not going to harm anything,' is the constant refrain when the owner of a high-energy large dog with a thousand times the power of smell of a human being is politely asked if it would be possible to retrieve the animal from the hedgerow and put him on a lead. 'He's got as much right to run around here as you have.' For the conservationist, one of the most painful consequences of the last few years, and particularly of Covid, has been a huge increase in the number of dogs – a significant proportion of them owned by people who either don't know or don't care about the damage they can do, particularly in the nesting season. Britain's depleted nature thus finds itself dealing with 13 million[3] not very competent but very clumsy and noisy apex predators, and so continues its retreat into the places where even they won't go.

Gradually, as the first ten-year scheme bedded in and adapted to every new reality, the new landscape that it was designed to foster emerged out of the former prairie. By the time Alex's role was taken over by Sue Simpson in 2009, each hedge boasted a conservation headland strip of some ten to twelve metres, which at a stroke fully reinstated two legs of

Dick Potts's original three-legged stool (those of habitat and food source) and partially reinstated the third (protection from over-predation) by providing a measure of cover from airborne predators within which partridges could move around to find food and generally stretch their wings.

As Sue explains, once the various options are layered up, the trick is to see where the holes are and to fill them with (depending on what may be appropriate) grazing animals, even more hedges or different varieties of seed mixes, and then to wrap the whole thing around the cash crops, such as low-input spring barley, in the reduced fields. It is a remarkable feature of the 'middle-way' character of the Peppering project that the agricultural operations at the heart of it continue to be intensive and highly productive; some concessions are made, to be sure, such as not using farm machinery at night, but to a great extent the farm team is allowed to get on with it. The first key is good communication and planning. The second is that, within the structure of a long-term deal, things must never be allowed to stand still, because that is the one thing nature never does; and there must always be a period of planning at least eighteen months before the implementation of something new. And the third key is even simpler: that of aiming for maximum variety at every turn, because it is variety, far more than any specific species, that tends to be the driver of increased biodiversity. Ironically, much of Natural England's recent work has been undoing actions that landowners had taken over the years because that is what the government had asked them to do, such as the grubbing out of hedges and the drying out of wetlands.

And although all parties have become better and more efficient at deciding on and then implementing the right schemes, there is no disguising the workload that the Peppering team,

The Return of the Grey Partridge

especially Peter Knight and farm secretary Sue Kennard, are obliged to put in. Equally, it is increasingly the experience gained from the hours spent on this work that has started to enable the team to spread the message further and wider, to a variety of estates that fancy going down the same route themselves.

Happily, it turns out that renaturing is catching.

As the hedges prospered and widened, so the biodiversity continued to seep back in.

That day in 2002 when Dick Potts had driven down to Arundel to inform Eddie of the parlous state of things for the few remaining grey partridges up on the western end of the Downs, Eddie had hardly dared to believe that he might one day be able to shoot wild partridges on his own land. Even in the early days of beetle banks and Sandringham deliveries, of Dick's glowing annual reports and of a sky full of birds, he had not allowed himself to imagine for too long that there might one day be a shootable surplus. The journey back from near local extinction is a long and arduous one and is by no means guaranteed to be successful. Remove the worst influences of man, and you are still faced with the lottery of disease and extreme weather. After all, it's not only since the Industrial Revolution that a soaking wet June has been more than the greys can cope with.

And yet, and yet, by the time the 2009 harvest had been gathered in, it became increasingly clear from the stubble-counts in the individual fields that this point had been reached, even exceeded. Dick Potts had always made it clear that, while he recognised and supported the idea that shooting was the driver of the natural miracle that was unfolding at Peppering, he did not want to be part of the decision as to when to go ahead with a full day of driven shooting. Everyone on the estate – Eddie included – understood that a man who had spent forty

Forty Years On

years drawing the nation's attention to the crisis facing grey partridges was entitled to be a bit ambivalent when it came to starting to kill some of them. So it was ultimately a decision between Eddie and the new head keeper, Tom Goodridge, who agreed to set up what would be the first day of driven wild partridges at Peppering for more than forty years. Tom quickly realised that no one in the area had ever been a beater or a flanker for wild birds on this terrain, meaning that it had every prospect of being more like herding cats than being the well-oiled military exercise it once was, and eventually became again. Besides, the hedges on the Peppering and Home Farm part of the land were still in their infancy and would be little or no use to a tall shooter trying to look inconspicuous.

Ironically, in a world where most gamekeepers long none too secretly for a few of their neighbours' birds to carelessly make their way over their own boundaries and thus bump up the bag, Eddie and Tom were extremely keen that no reared birds leaked in from the land to the east and to the north. If this was about anything, it was about wildlife, with the emphasis on the word 'wild'. The dream that drove the initial project, and still drives it now, was that every single bird shot at Peppering would be wild, with no room at all for anything reared to become involved, accidentally or otherwise. The only pheasants that congregate in the clearings and field edges at Peppering are smaller, sleeker and wilder than plump reared ones – more of a challenge to both shooter and predator alike. One of the seeming anomalies of the renaturing exercise at Peppering has been the team's strong and counter-intuitive dislike of stray reared birds that other keepers would be only too happy to play host to. What is run as an end-of-season beaters' day here would count as a much sought-after commercial let day elsewhere.

The date was set for 12 October 2009, a month away, and

invitations were despatched to the four guests who would join Eddie and his son, Henry. It speaks volumes for the respect with which Peter's endless work on the project was regarded that he himself was one of the guests at what would be the only shoot of the year, and it was by a country mile the biggest invitation he had received in his life. And it was with more than a cursory nod to history that Tom, along with Andrew Stringer and Beau Witney, the two beat keepers, unwrapped with some pride their new estate tweeds for the occasion. In attendance was a small contingent of expert flankers from Norfolk, who had come down to help, seasoned observers of grey partridge behaviour, who carried with them a professional knowledge of how to 'turn' a bird. Turning the bird – a technique of using flags to change the direction of the partridges – up in the folds and mounds of the landscape, was critical to the success of the whole operation.

Thus, behind hedges that were still under construction, and in front of a line of beaters and flankers who were very much learning on the job, the six guns lined up under the bright sunshine of that Monday morning. The initial drive was, appropriately enough, alongside the first of the new beetle banks and hedges below Canada Barn, which Peter and Nick had established some six years before. If the idea was initially more about proving concept than providing a traditional day's driven shooting, that concept found itself proved beyond argument by the star-burst of the very first covey about ten minutes into the drive, an explosion of grey partridges into all parts of the morning air as the hedge line was crossed and the first shot was fired, rather appropriately, by the man who had largely paid for it all up until that point.

'I wonder what that bird cost him,' murmured one of the beaters to his neighbour as the bird fell to the ground. They were words from one countryman to another, more a mark of respect for the endless endeavour and expense that had brought them all to this point rather than envy, disapproval or any such emotion. Whatever else had brought the greys back, it was not luck. And whatever else kept them there from now on, it wouldn't be economy.

As the day wore on, the standard of the birds simply became better and better. If the beat keepers and flankers had to learn as they went along, the same need not have been said for the partridges, into whose brains and central nervous system it seemed to be genetically wired exactly how to fly over what sort of terrain, how fast and how to react to the sight of a human being under the flight path. 'It was as if', noted one of the guns many years later, 'they had never been away.'

By lunch there was a general agreement that it was going as well as anyone had dared hope. As on most estates, matters run in the family, and Nick Field's mother, Libby, had been recruited to supply the shooting lunch; already nearly seventy years old, she would go on doing this for the best part of the next decade, come rain or shine. She, of all people, knew in her bones how important this was – not only to the Duke, but to everyone involved, her son very much included. Libby had regularly seen Nick up in the milking parlour long before daybreak so that he could get up to Peppering and work, and he had told her all about it in his occasional tea stopovers. In fact, they'd all talked about little else for weeks, and she had been on the farm for almost half a century, since Nick's father had tempted her away from her own family farm near Horsham to the dairy that she now called home. Old enough to have known small fields and miles of hedges before, Libby was happy to see them back and to be able to walk again among the wildlife they offered. Anyway, she was used to the more arduous routines of milking and carting hay (she once moved more than 1,000 bales in a day with her daughter), so providing cream of mushroom soup, crusty bread and flapjacks was well within her compass.

'Once you counted the keepers, beaters and pickers-up,' she remembers, 'I reckon I was catering for about sixty, all up. I knew most of them, from on or around the farm, but I loved that they came in from all parts of the country, all in their smart estate tweeds, all with this sense of purpose. Wherever you would find a partridge shoot, that's where they came from. In the event, most of them just wanted cream of mushroom soup, which became my speciality, I suppose; but there were always some who wouldn't touch it, so I either gave them oxtail or curried chicken and vegetable as the choice. You only try serving pumpkin soup the once up at Peppering.' She smiles at the memory.[4]

But what she remembers most of all is the sense of shared endeavour and achievement; the sense that this mattered not only to the people shooting, beating and picking up, but to the whole ecosystem of the farm. Eddie had hung his metaphorical hat on making this project work, on bringing the wild partridges back, and no one was deluding themselves that it didn't matter much if it didn't.

One of the tragedies of modern game-shooting is that it has all too often become a numbers game, a multiplication of a cost per presented bird by an agreed price, with an acceptable allowance for how often people are allowed to miss. The effect of this is to maximise the pressure on the head keeper to work against, rather than alongside, nature, and to saturate the ground with more reared birds than it is in the ground's capacity to hold. Looking at the thank-you letters for that first Peppering shoot a decade or so later, it is noteworthy that not one person mentioned, or probably even remembered, how many birds had been shot, because the numbers were simply not what it was about. The game book simply records that a few more French partridges than greys were shot, which was fine, and that two-thirds of the greys were young birds, which was probably less so. Instead, the letters talk about the delights of 'the unkempt hedges and organic grasses, the wild flowers and the wide headlands', and the opinion that Eddie had 'started a movement'. 'Wonderful sport,' said one, 'and for me a flashback to a quality of sport which I had long presumed would never be experienced again.' 'I think', said another, after a later shoot, 'that I have just glimpsed the future of shooting.'

The final letter came from Buckingham Palace, where the donor of those original nine pairs of grey partridges had got to hear, via the gamekeeper network, all about the success of the day. Alone among the others, the Duke of Edinburgh wanted to know all about the numbers as, to an extent, it was the only yardstick by which he could define the success (or otherwise) of the enterprise. 'Congratulations,' the letter said. 'It is very rewarding that all the effort – and cost – eventually pays off. The record is bound to be in numbers as there is, sadly, no other way of registering the sheer pleasure and excitement of shooting wild partridges.'

Up to a point, but only up to a point.

Peppering would be about many things. It would about the quality of the soil and the water that underpinned everything; about the variety of the plant and flower life, and the way the fields between the headlands were farmed; about the quantity of the invertebrates that made their living on the returning flora; and about the sky full of birds that fed on them. It would be about the raptors above the margins of the fields, and the mammals below them in the hedgerows. It would be about the farmers, contractors, shepherds, office staff, keepers and beat keepers, and about Peter and Eddie. But it would never be about the numbers. Not then, and not now.

In a way it was the relentless search for numbers that had brought British nature to its current depressing point in the first place. And, ironically, the notion that huge commercial days were the best way of creating a profitable and sustainable shoot was the exact thing that threatened the future of shooting itself.

A year later and there was a new head keeper.

Charlie Mellor had previously been a young beat keeper on Home Farm and had attracted positive attention in the short time he had been there, before heading off for a life of surf and sand in Australia. After a year he had returned to England to collect the rest of his possessions and go back to the 'lucky country' for good; he was, after all, only in his mid-twenties and was far from decided about a long-term career. By way of earning some money while he was back, he took on some temporary work with the estate's fencing contractor, putting in fencing at the far north of Peppering, which was where Eddie found him one morning while he was out walking his dogs. It was exactly twenty-four hours after the planned new head keeper had handed in his notice.

'I can't work here,' the keeper had said. 'You've got people everywhere. Footpaths everywhere. Dogs everywhere. I just can't do it.' He had come down from Northumberland, where you could go for a week without seeing anyone, and he didn't appreciate the general busyness of the south. Whatever else he was going to do, it did not involve going about his work among walkers.

There was little point sitting around and wondering

whether the keeper couldn't have worked this all out for himself ahead of his long trip south. However, his departure, and its timing, presented Eddie and Peter with a major problem, with the additional unlikelihood that any keeper good enough and experienced enough to take on this kind of role would be prepared to come over at such short notice.

'I'm collecting my stuff and then I'm back off to Australia,' said Charlie, when Eddie asked him what he doing back in the area. In the twenty minutes it took Eddie to walk home, he thought the unthinkable. On the one hand, Charlie was only twenty-six and had never had anything like this responsibility; on the other hand, he was a high-quality operator with a deep knowledge of the ecology of the estate and a lifelong passion for grey partridges. Once Eddie had ascertained that Peter didn't think he was out of his mind, he asked the contractor to see if Charlie wouldn't mind coming down to the estate office as soon as possible. At that stage Eddie didn't even have Charlie's mobile number.

Fifteen minutes later, with Charlie's muddy quad-bike still steaming in the car park, he was offered the job.

'It's a learning process for all of us,' said Eddie. 'You'll have lots of ideas and energy. You'll make mistakes, of course, but as long as we all learn from them, we'll back you.'

Three minutes later he had a new head keeper for the Peppering shoot who was not yet thirty years old, and Charlie was earnestly trying to get his money back on an economy ticket to Sydney.

There was a postscript.

In the stubble-counts the following September, Eddie was able to report to the judging panel of the annual Purdey Awards for Game and Conservation that there were now 2,150 grey partridges on the ground where once there had been five, of which no fewer than 1,290 were on the new land that had been in hand for just four years.

This was important. A month earlier the panel had sent Eddie a letter in which, after due praise for the estate's submission, it was advised that their entry be deferred by a year, so that the results of one more shooting season could be included. The disclosure of the new figures, it was felt, would absolutely put to bed any uncertainty the judges harboured about the extent of the estate's ability to provide a good quantity of high-quality birds. Besides, nothing in the way Eddie had conducted matters in the last decade suggested that he would be patient. As he himself would point out on many occasions, the state of British nature simply did not allow for timidity and patience. The urgency meant that continual action was needed, even if that meant, as it sometimes did, the unsubtle removal of the obstacles that were strewn in its way.

The Purdey Award was important. Not so much for the £5,000 winner's cheque, which wouldn't put much more than a dent in one month of costs of the operation, but for the peer-reviewed approval that it consigned, and the knowledge that what the estate had done had been benchmarked against the best. And, in this game, the best were very good indeed.

A few days later the Peppering Estate was announced as the winner, and on 18 November 2010 Eddie, Peter, Charlie, Andrew and Beau went up to receive their award from the previous year's winner, the Duke of Northumberland, at Purdey's Long Room in central London. By receiving the award personally from another landowner with an obsession with grey partridges, a signal was perhaps also being sent to the remainder of the shooting community that this was a cause very much worth fighting for. From now on, the challenge would need to evolve and go on to demonstrate, to the widest possible audience, that you didn't have to be from the landed gentry, or have unfeasibly deep pockets, to do the right thing by the wildlife on your farm.

One by one the guests departed, until it was just the Peppering team left, being gently shoehorned towards the exit.

'Getting my three keepers in full kit in through the barriers at Victoria Station on the way up there was one thing,' remembers Peter Knight of the evening. 'Getting them back through a few hours later was quite another.'

The Peppering partridge manor was well and truly back in action.

PART TWO
Now

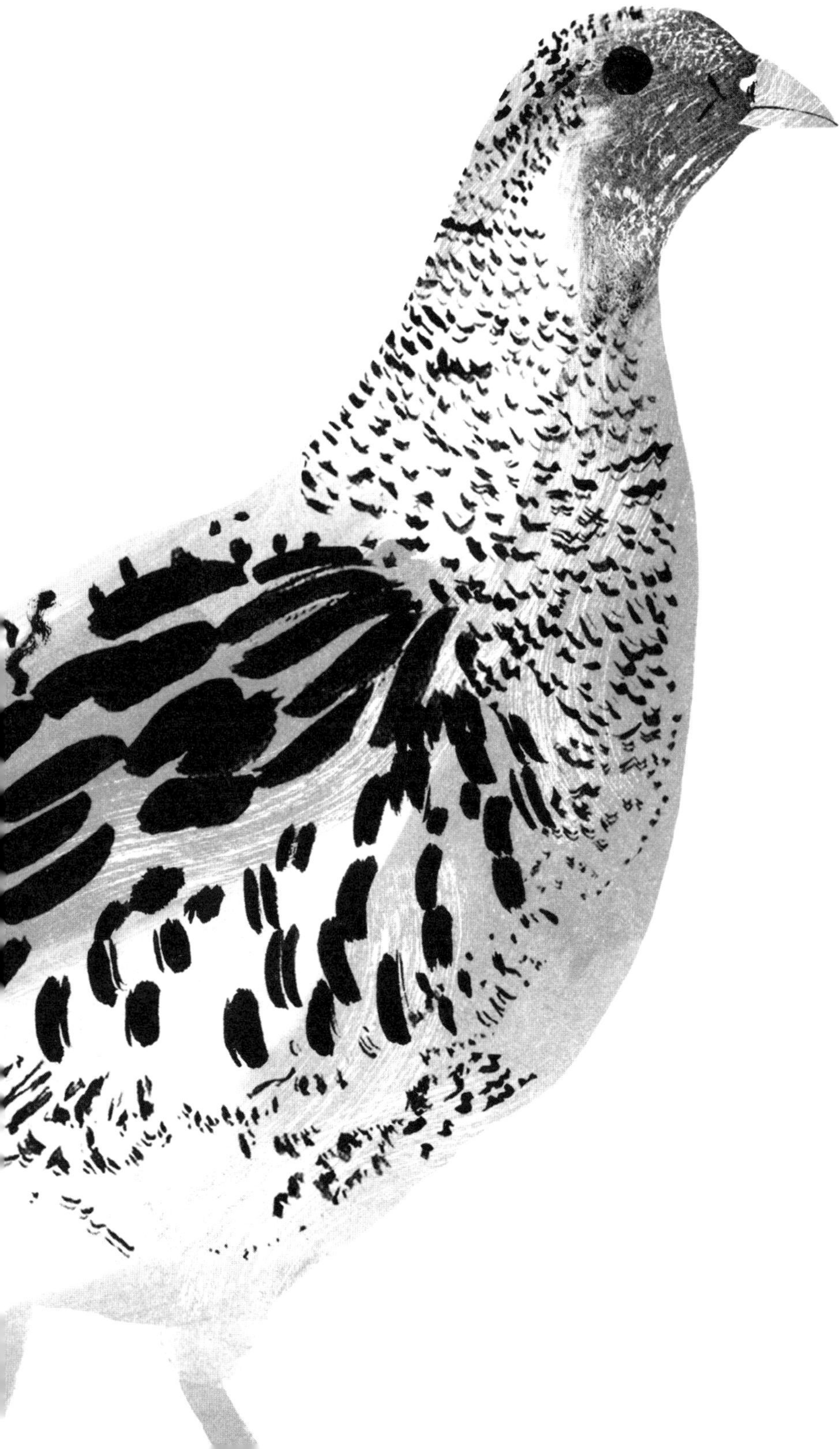

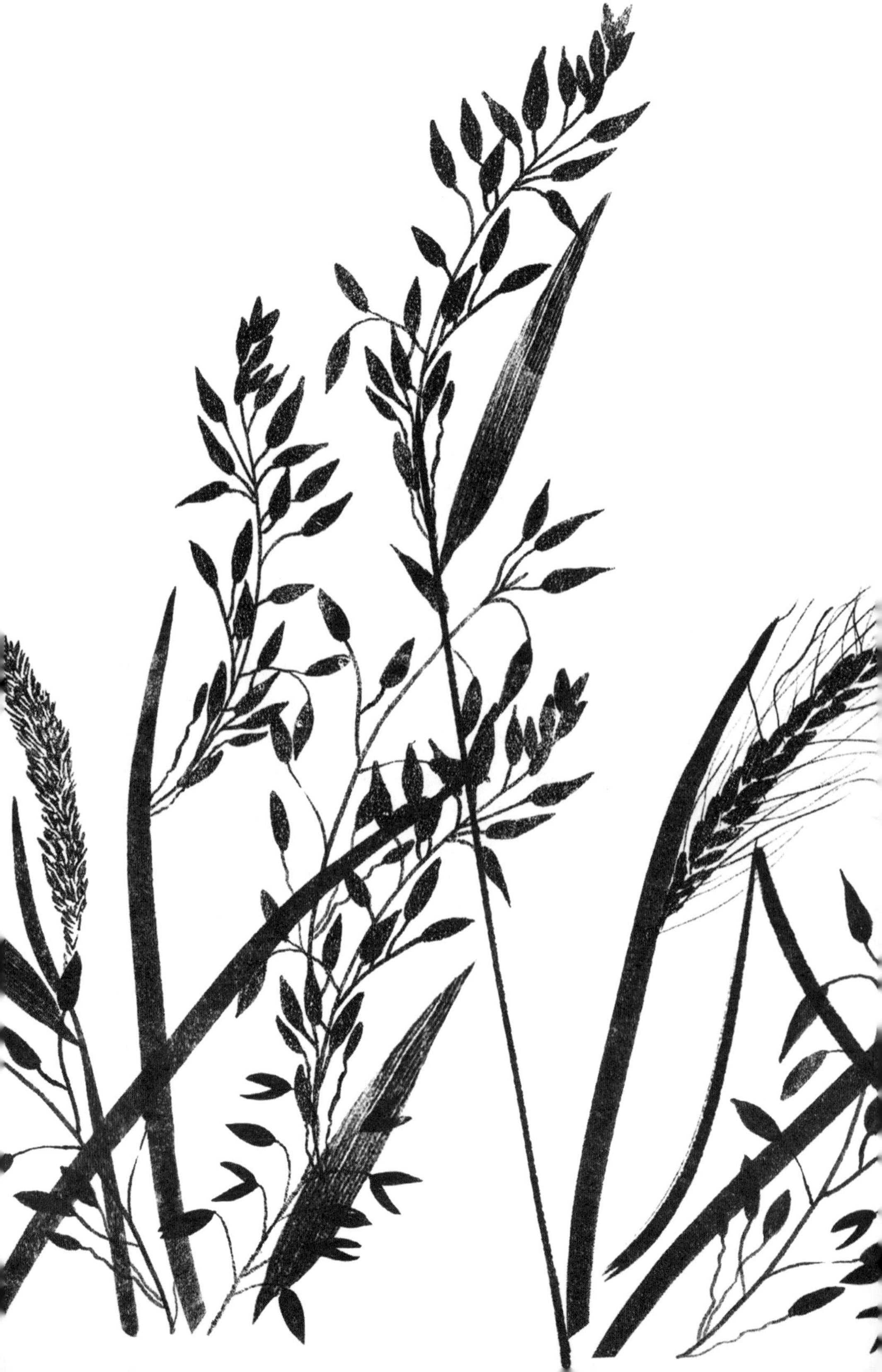

6

FARMING FOR BIODIVERSITY: EARLY SPRING

'Believe it or not, there's more that unites us than divides us,' says farm manager Conor Haydon with a smile.

He is standing over a table that is covered with a large multi-coloured map of the estate. On the other side of the table is head keeper Charlie Mellor, and this meeting is part of an ongoing twelve-month conversation between the two of them as to how the land is to be farmed, and run, over the coming year. It is twenty years since the patchwork-quilt multi-crop approach was introduced to the estate, before either man was in full-time work, let alone at Peppering, and this map shows the scheme in all its coded colours: red for winter wheat, blue for winter barley, purple for peas, yellow for spring barley, green for grass and blue for winter beans.

Conor's comment is a subtle nod to what others might think to be the underlying, mutually incompatible aims between what each is paid to do on the farm, where the needs of biodiversity and the welfare of the grey partridge place consistent constraints on the freedom with which the farm manager can go about his business of maximising yields and returns. In fact, maintaining this healthy and sometimes delicate balance between food production and stewardship has been an integral part of the formula for the success of the Peppering project since its earliest days. Without Charlie and Conor understanding the realities of the pressures on the other, the process would have been a long and tedious round of explanation and negotiation. Without them working together, neither of them would have worked at all.

'For a start, we both happen to work for a boss who accords roughly equal priority to profitable food production and the grey partridge shooting, which makes it much easier. He sees farming as an integral part of the mission of the estate, which is unusual in the shooting world. Many just pay it lip service. And equally, he sees shooting as an integral backdrop to the way we farm, from the hedgerows and field sizes, right down to the time of day we harvest. Secondly, it is a fluid process that can, and will, change as different decisions are made or come up for review. So there is never a sense of either side winning. In fact, there is never a sense of sides at all. We both make an effort to understand each other's work and, at the end of the day, we both know that we have been employed to manage the land for biodiversity as well as profit.'

The farming is hard here, certainly in comparison with the fertile coastal plain a few miles to the south. Very little of it is flat, and what is flat has some of the thinnest soil cover of all. A thick layer of sloping chalk with a weak layer of topsoil between two and twenty centimetres thick is no medium in which to conduct intensive wheat or vegetable production, so the land is instead divided up into grain crops and sheep, their allotted spaces parcelled up, in Conor's annual multicoloured cropping plan, in rotation. The poverty of the soil also helps to explain why between one-third and half of the annual harvest from the farm goes into feed for animals, as opposed to food for humans.

The rotational period is four or five years, depending on

Farming for Biodiversity: Early Spring

how you measure it. Starting with winter wheat (which has high margins, but is prone to accumulate disease if grown for a second or third year), it moves on in phase two to winter barley, with the harvest going into animal feed, followed by spring barley, which goes into malting. The final phase is winter beans or a cover crop, or occasionally two years of grass. Sometimes turnips are slotted in between winter wheat and spring barley to give the lambs something to get fat on, in readiness for the spring market.

'We used to grow oilseed rape,' says Conor, 'but the input costs needed on such marginal land make it much too expensive at the moment, so we have stopped it completely.' The same applies to peas, once a staple crop at Peppering, but now a loss-maker even in a good year. Again this is a function of the coefficient of high costs and low market price. Over and over again, the biggest single factor for Conor is the marginal land he is responsible for. And over and over again it is land that he is seeking to improve, whether by an ongoing process of testing sample fields for worm counts, potassium and sodium, organic matter and even the pH levels or by the additions he makes to it. He may be young, but Conor is a traditional enough farmer to appreciate when a flock of common gulls follows the plough, because he knows they wouldn't do it if there were not a number of worms being turned over onto the surface.

'At the end of the day, it all has to pay,' he explains, 'and often what we do, and when we do it, just comes down to the maths. If I have got to put in 800 acres of spring barley to a certain deadline, which should eventually yield around 1,800 tons at harvest, Charlie knows that is around £300,000 of income for the business, which explains to him, before I need to, why I might be a little late sowing his conservation headlands.'

In simplistic terms, the main farming change around here

is that around 15 per cent of the land has been taken out of food production as the source of its main financial contribution to the estate and slotted into stewardship schemes instead. Twenty years ago the farm consisted of thirty-eight huge fields, all more or less ploughed up to the edge and subject to the usual chemical additives of the day. The price of easy farming, as Dick Potts had so clearly shown, was a biodiversity desert. These days, with ninety-five fields, the work has to be in lockstep with the needs of ground-nesting birds, which means one crop being spread far and wide over, say, five different fields in different parts of the farm, whereas once it had all been in the same place. That, in turn, means having to move equipment around further and more often, a little erosion of efficiency and more communication between the various workers on the estate. Spraying is fine – this is not an organic enterprise, after all – but its application has to be rigorously controlled, so that not one drop goes onto the neighbouring conservation headland. And when other farms work deep into the night in summer months, here everything stops at last light, so as to avoid the accidental crushing of a grey partridge.

Ironically, perhaps the biggest sacrifice that an organised farmer like Conor has to make here is in the general neatness of the place – tidiness being the enemy of biodiversity, just as much as unsuitable land use. As a naturally ordered man, one of the many concessions he has to make to the nature threaded richly through his farm is to suppress his instinct to tidy the place up.

Charlie explains how, in contrast to the prevailing creative tensions, there are also many ways in which the two teams can actively help each other. 'A number of the jobs that the beat keepers have to do are made a lot easier by borrowing the relevant farm machinery, for example; just as my guys going out and controlling serious outbreaks of rabbit or pigeon overpopulation is great for Conor. Ditto deer. Ditto rats, but even more so, particularly around the buildings. Rats are the bane of all of our lives round here.'

One area where both sets of interests have been served by the same end has been the recent introduction of commercial wild pheasant days on the Peppering Estate. As we learned earlier, the pheasant is a bird more tolerated than welcomed on the Peppering Estate, mainly due to its propensity to scare grey partridges away from feeders (which, in turn, makes the greys more likely to be predated, by searching for alternative food out in the open) or to trample its eggs. As anyone who has shot either will freely tell you, a wild pheasant is an altogether more challenging – and therefore potentially more valuable – game bird than the reared one, so much so that a day can be let out for £100 a bird. All the wild birds will probably have been descended from ones originally reared on one of the neighbouring shoots, but, through fending for themselves for food and protecting themselves from predators, they tend to be sleeker, quicker, faster and more manoeuvrable than their penned cousins. Most shooters would agree that they need rather fewer of the former than the latter, to constitute a good day's sport. These birds will fly much better from cover that has been managed and controlled over the year, than from thick, dense cover, where they can simply run away from dogs and never take off, a land management service that the farming side of the business could supply. In turn, the £20,000 income from the let day of, say, 200 birds, helps to offset the high costs of the shooting operation. The height and density of cover crops pay an important part in driving grey partridges as well, so what is good for one activity tends to be good for both.

Because the farming and shooting are run as part of one

business, both elements have a keen interest in doing the right thing by the other. In good years the whole business can show a reasonable profit; in others (2021, for example), even the prevailing strong prices for lambs failed to compensate for the effects of a cold, dry spring and a long, wet summer on both the arable product and the availability of pheasants and partridges to sell for field sports. Annoyingly, a wet June is bad for just about everything on the estate, and wet Junes happen to be one of the features of our changing climate.

Most of the principles that are applied to regenerative farming are already followed at Peppering, although it is a broad-brush term that Conor thinks can be misleading, and which he therefore avoids. The fifth of those principles – bringing grazing animals back to the land – is observed through the now-familiar Romney sheep dotted all over the estate, chosen originally because a neighbour had a successful breeding flock that gave them the confidence, and the raw material, to give it a go themselves. The 1,600 or so ewes tend to graze the steeper ground that has been given over to permanent pasture, unsuitable for any arable activity, which makes up about half of the available grassland at any one point in the rotation. These are looked after by two full-time shepherds, including running the entire lambing process out on the hill; 2,500 lambs make their way into the food chain over the winter and early spring, part of a contract-at-one-remove to supply one of the UK's 'smarter' supermarket chains.

'The shepherds have an important part to play, beyond looking after the sheep,' Conor says. 'They are out all hours, and will notice things that even the beat keepers might not always see. They contribute by doing something as simple as remembering to avoid driving down the headland tracks where the snares have been set, all the way to letting us know of predator levels on certain parts of the farm.' Above all, at lambing time, they have to be on the lookout for dogs straying off the footpaths and worrying the stock.

Those shepherds, along with one full-time tractor driver, represent the entire employed staff on the farm. The rest of the work is done by long-term contractors, spearheaded by Nick Field, who has been in on the project since before Conor and Charlie were on the payroll – before they even left school, in fact. The fact that Nick's 'other' job is to run his own herd of dairy cattle, which theoretically only requires his attention under normal circumstances at either end of the working day, means that he is largely available to do daytime work on the estate and that he rarely has a day off or begins one later than five in the morning.

'I get it,' says Nick of what is happening on the land above his own dairy. 'If I wasn't fully signed up to the grey partridge project, much of what I do up there wouldn't make any sense at all. But I am, so it does.'

Looking after 1,600 ewes is not something that can be contracted out, like the harvest. It is a twelve-month intensive job with plenty of attendant risk and not much let-up, which means that Martin Pimm the resident head-shepherd, is indirectly an influential part of the team that runs the estate and delivers the results.

Mainly he grazes his sheep out on the permanent pasture or on the two-year grass leys but, when the time is right, he also moves them through the cover crops and stubble turnips, grazing in narrow strips until they have eaten everything down to the required level and are ready to move on. Not to the extent of a cow perhaps, but sheep are still biodiversity engineers, always working their hungry way around the farm, week by week, temporary fence by temporary fence, keeping the grass down and helping out in the preparation of the cropping plan. They also represent a valuable income stream for the farm, not through the wool (which, being virtually valueless these days, is more about welfare than money), but through the lamb entering the food chain some time between July and March, depending on the maturity of the animal.

But the axis on which Martin's year rotates is lambing, which generally takes place throughout March. 'They call what we do "easy lambing",' he says with a wry smile. By 'easy lambing', they mean getting the job done naturally, out on the hill, rather than back in a lambing shed. 'You get used to it, though. It's so weather-dependent, that's the problem. Wet newborn lambs need attention straight away, as do the triplets.' Recently Martin has introduced a proportion of Hampshire rams into the breeding mix, to create even more suitability for the downland environment.

In many ways, running the sheep alongside the shoot works well for the sheep. After all if they weren't controlled by the keepers, 1,600 ewes would attract a lot of foxes around lambing time, which could do considerable damage.

'Actually, ravens are the new key predator round here, as far as I am concerned,' says Martin. 'It's like they've come into the area almost overnight but, however they arrived, they are remorseless, particularly on the first lamb of twins or triplets. Straight at the belly and the eyes. Nothing we can do, apart from put crow-scarers up around the lambing fields.'

Ravens are a good example of the complexities often hidden within successful renaturing. On the one hand, who could not thrill to the sight and sound of Britain's largest corvid returning to the Downs after so many decades of absence? On the other, the raven is a highly successful opportunist, high up in the food

Farming for Biodiversity: Early Spring

chain, which not only nests high and early, but also makes plans and remembers things, meaning that it can be a devastating predator among the ground-nesting birds, which, like the grey partridge, may only recently have returned themselves.

The shooting itself is no more than a small seasonal complication in Martin's working year, a question of making sure the sheep aren't in the wrong place on shoot day. 'Partridges don't like to fly over livestock,' he says, 'so I need to know where the drives are in advance, and make sure that the sheep don't end up between the guns and the beaters. Put it this way: I'd rather get a polite call from Charlie a few days before the shoot than an upset one immediately after it!'

Over the years, both pigs and cattle have occasionally been considered as an addition to the mix, but both have been rejected on the respective grounds of too much management and too much potential trouble. It's one thing, after all, when a flock of sheep breaks through a temporary fence, but quite another when a herd of conservation cattle gets out from where they are supposed to be, into somewhere with greater fragility and sensitivity. Equally, the corollary to hosting a large number of pigs would be a rapid acceleration in the number of the very crows, rooks and jackdaws the beat keepers have been trying to control. Over recent years, however, the farm has imported about 5,000 tonnes of pig manure annually from a nearby herd, so as to help increase the general levels of nitrogen where they are too low. The cost – at around £10 a tonne after delivery and spreading – compares favourably to the cost of the compound fertiliser that would otherwise have to be used, on top of which it is a source of phosphate, potash, zinc and other trace elements. Conor can see the day coming when the farm starts to use sewage sludge, a more concentrated but even more regulated version of manure, but concedes that some things take longer than others to get used to, within the culture of an organisation.

'I think it will happen,' he says. 'But not any time soon.'

As we saw in Chapter 3, at least 10 per cent of the farm's annual income comes from one or more of Natural England's stewardship schemes. While this doesn't exactly define the business, it is nonetheless a very influential part of it. Crucially, it is also one that has the benefit of being guaranteed from the minute it is entered into, which is very much more than can be said for the financial outcomes that derive from cereal or livestock activities. Phase by phase and year by year, the various conservation disciplines will subtly change. This is not so much to chase the money – although that is always going to be an important factor in a system where, for example, a hectare of unharvested headland attracts 150 per cent more grant than one that is harvested – as to maintain the sense of holistic and joined-up land management over a protracted period of time.

Recently the farm has also been able to benefit from a separate scheme. It is run by the local water utility, and the farm is paid £120 per hectare to take some of the catchment ground out of production over a protracted period, either with a cover crop or just grass, so as to reduce the long-term flow of nitrates and other inputs downstream to the purification stage. In this way, what the water company spends in 2020 by way of a subsidy to Peppering, it saves in 2030 by the time the water has worked its slow way through the chalk aquifers and has arrived at the treatment stage. Once he factors in the £55 a hectare tractoring costs that the sheep will save him, through grazing down the cover crop and leaving the remainder of it in the ground as green manure, Conor feels that he is well up on

Farming for Biodiversity: Early Spring

the deal and has better ground, with more nitrogen fixed, and more organic content to the soil. And on the estate Charlie is happy, because he has more ground suitable for his partridges, and Conor knows in advance exactly what financial return he can expect for the thirty or so hectares involved.

It's yet another good example of a basic truth that underpins the whole project: for all the planning, commitment, borrowing and private investment, the Peppering project would not have lasted twenty years, or achieved the extraordinary biodiversity gains it has, without the background financial commitment of the estate to the long process of starting to right the ecological wrongs of the previous century. Eddie is more than aware that he has had the personal financial headroom to do all this and to be the one doing the experimenting. Equally, he is adamant that the future renaturing of farming does not have to be exclusively a rich person's game.

And in this game, planning and predictions are one thing, but what actually happens on the day, on the ground, can sometimes be quite another. In the spring of 2022, for example, two potentially seismic influences came to bear on Conor and on all his planning: one local, and one from far away. The local one was the proposed laying of the second phase of power cables from the enormous £1.3 billion Rampion offshore wind farm, visible out in the English Channel a few miles off the coast, which could blaze a fifty-metre-wide swathe across the land that had taken twenty years to gift back to nature. Rampion provides clean power to around one-third of a million homes, so it is of national importance, and its cables have to go somewhere; equally, Peppering risked losing large chunks of fields from its farm planning, and even more significant chunks of hedgerow from its biodiversity plan. There was a painstaking and delicate negotiation to be had.

The far-away influence was the effect of the Russian invasion of Ukraine, a country that normally produces one-fifth of all global high-grade wheat, and 7 per cent of all global wheat. Suddenly and with no warning, Conor's input costs rocketed upwards, but so too did the potential price of his wheat and barley. Delicate sums on the balance between stewardship income and farm sales, painstakingly worked out in the winter by Conor and Sue, became meaningless in the face of a commodity price that had doubled. Every headland, previously washing its face in the stewardship income it attracted, was now a missed opportunity to make money for the farm.

Conor knows many farmers who have simply walked away from any such schemes, simply to get back into full and profitable food production, even when the cost is borne by the local biodiversity. 'We're lucky,' he says, looking out at the wheeling lapwings on a spring cover crop of peas and radish. Lapwing pairs on the estate are up to thirty-two, from nineteen the previous year, a statistic that he knows derives from the way he farms. 'We bought most of this year's inputs ahead, and therefore at last year's prices. At the same time, we sold futures in our wheat and barley, so we can't ride the upside to its full extent. But from next year we are in the full glare of the market, for good and bad.'

Peppering is lucky in that its owner has the will and, importantly, the resources to take a longer view on this, and for the time being the wildlife is safe. But if the war becomes a wider European one, then it could well be that those hedgerows get grubbed up again by government diktat, for the second time in under a century.

'It's something I've only just started thinking about again, really,' says Conor. 'Our obligation, as farmers, to feed the world.'

Farming for Biodiversity: Early Spring

At Peppering, as in the ministries in London, much of this is not much more complicated than an agreement and a determination to allow nature back into farming. 'Allowing' nature back onto a farm is an almost insulting concept that would have had our ancestors scratching their heads in confusion, but that doesn't make it any less real. We are lucky that, for the most part, nature is resilient and floods back in when the conditions are right.

We might mourn that this has had to be so, but at least we can now start to celebrate some of nature's achievements, and the fact that once again it is mainstream. It is not rewilding so much as regeneration; not isolated blocks of plenty so much as interconnected corridors of vibrant wildlife potential.

7

PREDATOR CONTROL: LATE SPRING

After a time the sense of amazement and newness started to abate.

The intense period of rebuilding that had followed Dick Potts's visit to the estate office back in 2002 had, to a certain extent, come to an end with the first twenty-eight grams of lead shot leaving Eddie's gun on the morning of 12 October 2009. If everything before that day had been built around simply enabling it to happen (as unlikely as that eventuality must have seemed, back in the early days), from then on it would have to be about the maintenance and gradual improvement of the ecosystem as a matter of daily routine because, just as nature had seeped strongly back in, it could equally quickly seep back out again if the damaging habits were allowed to return.

By and large, the annual counts done by Dick Potts continued to show a steady strengthening in the overall return of nature to the hill. In 2014 he delightedly reported on the highest insect abundance so far, which was, he said 'almost entirely due to the extraordinary abundance of blossom beetles'; and the best wintering bird returns since they had begun to record them, particularly of the skylark. The same year he noticed that the field vole was rapidly increasing in numbers, a sure sign that barn-owl and kestrel populations would rise alongside them. At the same time his censuses demonstrated that, for all the conservation work put in on their behalf, some species

Predator Control: Late Spring

simply declined in certain years, normally for reasons beyond the control of scientists or field workers: in the same year that insects had generally thrived, grasshoppers were struggling, yellowhammers had halved in number and they had only seen one cornflower all year. There would continue to be good years and bad years,[1] triumphs and disasters, but the aim would never change from being the production of a reasonable harvestable surplus of utterly wild grey partridges, and all the associated biodiversity gains that went hand in hand with that.

And no part of that routine would be as critical as the legal, costly and, above all, relentless control of predators.

Not everything in game management is as straightforward, or as uncontroversial, as habitat creation and the supply of food. The third element of Dick Potts's three-legged stool, the legal control of predators, has been a crucial element in the return of the grey to the South Downs, just as it has been in the toolbox of humans since the time of the ancient Sumerians 4,500 years ago. We need to travel two or three steps back in the workings of a standard ecosystem to see why this might be, and why it all starts with the absence of apex predators.

To understand the role that apex predators, or the lack of them, might have played in the gradual extinction of the grey partridge at Peppering, we can do worse than start by heading 4,500 miles west to Yellowstone National Park in the state of Wyoming.

Back in the 1920s the last Yellowstone wolf had been shot, an absence that had led directly to the resident elk – freed from the climate of fear that the wolves had imposed – evolving a more leisurely and much more environmentally damaging grazing habit, especially down by the rivers. What had once been a highly mobile winter grazer now stayed in one place for long periods of time, especially in the winter, to trash the young willow, sallow and cottonwood plants, primary food sources for the beaver, whose numbers quickly declined into the low double figures in consequence.

Between 1995 and 1997, and only after two decades of intense negotiation and persuasion, forty-one timber wolves were reintroduced to Yellowstone to start to rebalance the ecosystem. Once those wolves were released from their travel boxes and allowed to trot into the wide blue yonder, their presence set off a chain of events that reimposed a sense of nervousness among the elk, which, in turn, enabled the willows to thrive and then (among many other things) the beaver to come back in numbers, which created dams and pools, which attracted long-absent insects, which summoned back long-gone birds and small mammals, until an array of long-absent species had found their way back to Yellowstone, all because of the reintroduction of one apex predator. And because the wolves would also kill a good number of that junior predator, the coyote, while they were at it, there were downstream benefits for many other smaller mammals as well. There were downsides, of course, such as the occasional killing of livestock by the wolves, not to mention the feeling among hunters that something unwelcome was muscling in on their quarry, but as an exercise in demonstrating the process of 'trophic cascade,'[2] it has few equals.

Of course, Peppering is not Yellowstone, but the principle still applies that predators will always influence the prey population by acting as a top-down control and, in consequence, will go on to influence the landscape. Wolves and lynx haven't been seen in Sussex for half a millennium but, as we saw in Chapter 1, once that other hyper-apex predator – the gamekeeper – was largely removed after the First World War, the chief beneficiaries were the 'mesopredators', medium-sized hunters like the fox, stoat, buzzard and crow, and the unprotected prey populations below suffered. The predators could kill at will, and in increasing numbers, secure in the knowledge that little or nothing would come after them in return.

Nature relies on equilibrium being maintained, and the problem for the grey partridge (as it has been for the curlew and the hare, for example) has been one that ends up looking a lot like terminal decline. Healthy populations can sustain robust predation; a population already on its knees can't. This situation is exacerbated by the effects of around 50 million pheasants and partridges being released each year in the UK (only one-third of which end up being shot), which go on to act as a magnet for increased numbers of predators, which then go on to kill other ground-nesting birds. As one major conservation charity said in the introduction to its landmark report on predators: 'In most cases, it is human interventions that upset the balance of nature between the eaten and the eaters.'[3] True, but these days it is unfortunately also only human intervention that is able to put in place the pieces for recovery, at least to begin with.

Nonetheless, legal predator control is still, for many valid reasons, a highly emotive subject.[4] After all, the instinct of most people who are privileged enough to make their living in nature is to preserve biodiversity, not to restrict it. And it's not as if all the predator numbers are beyond future vulnerability: stoats and weasels, for instance, both of which can be legally controlled, each only have seasonal pre-breeding numbers of around half a million in the UK as it is,[5] slightly more than the fox. Corvids are currently more successful, with 1.1 million carrion-crow territories alone,[6] but many people still feel an instinctive discomfort at the idea of humans playing God in the prioritisation of which species lives and which dies. Or, indeed, at killing any of them. Unsurprisingly, it tends only to be when discussing our 150 million rats that a more general and positive consensus emerges about the need to control. All this is often the point of divergence between different conservation groups and individuals. While habitat improvement will always be hugely important in helping to sustain populations, many predator prevention measures – for example, electric fences around nest sites – have proved expensive, time-consuming and obviously ineffective against anything with wings. Other measures, such as diversionary feeding, removing potential breeding sites and perching places, can be useful, but are of relatively low impact.

So Dick Potts was adamant that continuous legal predator control was of equal importance in his three-legged stool with habitat and plentiful food, and he insisted that, without it, the grey partridge at Peppering would be no more. Neither Eddie nor Peter disagreed back then, and no one at Peppering disagrees now.

A young grey partridge emerging from its egg on the South Downs, or any ground-nesting bird for that matter, has an impressive array of potential diners to avoid if it is going to make its uncertain way to adulthood, and that is without counting the prevailing weather conditions, which, as we have seen already, can sink a breeding season without trace if they are cold and wet at the wrong time. This is nothing new. It has been this way since the dawn of time.

At the outset, and even when the chick is still in the relative safety of an egg deep in a nest-scrape in some hedge, there will be adders and grass snakes to contend with, not to mention opportunistic hedgehogs or grey squirrels, or even calcium-hungry sheep or deer. Other hazards to the partridge while still

Predator Control: Late Spring

in the egg come from hen pheasants and red-legged partridges moving through and kicking the eggs out of the nest, and from magpies, crows, rooks, jackdaws, jays and ravens. In fact, the only resident British corvid that does not pose a serious problem is the chough, and then only because it happens not to live within 150 miles of Peppering.

'We've even lost eggs to moles,' says Charlie, 'when they dig up through the soft earth below, and the eggs fall through the resulting hole in the bottom of the nest.' Then he concedes that this could just be a highly intelligent weasel using the tunnel that a mole has already prepared, to access some protein all the easier.

But it is once the chick is hatched that the predation begins in earnest, not least because something that is inside an egg has the temporary advantage of being silent and therefore hard to detect. The corvids will take a chick as gratefully as they would an egg, but now they are joined by the raptors – which are, ironically, thriving over the sympathetically farmed and carefully managed ground: kestrels, goshawks, red kites, peregrines, buzzards, marsh harriers, hen harriers and tawny owls. In the vanguard of all these is the relentless sparrowhawk, whose combination of speed and manoeuvrability gives it an extraordinary advantage when working a hedgerow or some stubble.

However, the attentive parent doesn't have the luxury of only looking up into the sky for danger. Far from it: along the hedgerow will come in turn weasels, stoats, mink, polecats and feral ferrets, members of the wider mustelid family, voraciously efficient hunters with excellent night vision and a powerful sense of smell. The omnivorous badger will welcome an evening meal of partridge chicks if it happens upon them, and urban foxes will routinely come all the way from Brighton

The Return of the Grey Partridge

(twenty miles to the east) to join the rural ones that are already in the area.

'We keep getting told that foxes are strictly territorial,' says Charlie Mellor, 'and that one good strong dog fox in the area will deter any others from coming in and working the ground. That is absolutely not our experience here. You only have to sit on a high seat with night-viewing equipment after dark, or listen to the stereophonic sound of vixens barking, or cubs complaining, to see how little they see it as a territory, and how much they see it as a convenient free-for-all fast-food outlet. We have a constant stream of both urban and rural foxes coming onto the estate night after night and creating havoc, not only with the partridges, but with hares, rabbits and anything else stuck on the ground.'

But that is not all. Add to that list some feral cats, plus a few domestic ones straying out from the local villages, and any number of dogs allowed by their owners to roam free along the hedges during the breeding season and we are missing only one predator from our eventual list of thirty-four.

That one is the rat, possibly the grey partridge's predator-in-chief, as it is so often with other species right across nature. And with its extraordinary capacity for self-multiplication (one pregnant female can give rise to 1,250 rats in a period of twelve months), an unerring nose for a food source, teeth that never stop growing and activity throughout the seasons, it is one that demands the keepers' attention all the time.

The list of predators looks impressive but, among healthy prey populations, even those thirty-four different species of hunter wouldn't be enough to start a long-term decline in a normal season. After all, the vast majority of them were just as influential as they are now, centuries before the baleful effects of *Homo sapiens* started to come into force.

Predator Control: Late Spring

In other words, legal predator control is only necessary in the first place in order to undo the damage that our own species has wrought. But the team finds it unquestionably necessary, and it is unquestionably humans who have to do it.

Of those thirty-four species, only ten fall into the category of being legal to control: basically most of the corvids, some of the mustelids and all of the foxes and rats. Feral cats are legal quarry as well, but can be vanishingly difficult to control. Of the corvids, the raven is subject to full protection, and rooks and jays can only be controlled if they are damaging crops and woodland bird populations respectively, which, in the case of Peppering, they clearly aren't. Which leaves only the crows and magpies.

In practical terms, the control can be done in one of four ways: trapping, snaring, shooting or poisoning. In all of these the Peppering staff are careful to follow whatever is industry best practice, in terms of the avoidance of unnecessary suffering, which, because it is a developing science, often means expensive upgrades right across the estate. On an estate that is running 750 tunnel traps, for example, all of which have just been superseded in terms of best practice by a new one that costs £38, the £28,000 replacement budget is not one that can be spread over many years; all the old ones have to be replaced as soon as possible.

As it is, the predator control season at Peppering starts at the end of shooting and continues until harvest.

'The countryside is a hungry place,' explains Charlie Mellor, 'especially in March.' This is a particular problem for a wild shoot like Peppering, where game is available to predators all year round, unlike many of the neighbouring shoots where it comes to an almost immediate end, a signal for a one-way stream of carnivores coming to try their luck up the hill. At this point a beat keeper becomes the equivalent of the timber wolf in Yellowstone, an apex predator in his own right, working his patch to ensure that a workable balance is maintained throughout the season.

Essentially the keeper achieves this by intercepting animals that are going about their general routines: a fox that is coming into the territory from a nearby town, using the same old existing tracks for convenience, for example; a stoat that is scouring the line of a hedgerow for an unwary bird; or a family of rats that has made camp underneath a convenient feeding hopper. Although the keepers have quad-bikes and Land Rovers to get them about, this process begins and ends on foot, with countless hours of observation, on ground they already know more precisely than their own kitchens, looking for a feather here, a thin, muddy track worn smooth or a fallen log with more than one set of footprints running up it.

'You end up thinking like an animal after a while,' says Andrew Stringer, back from seven years of retirement to take up his old beat again. 'A sort of natural detective.' It's a process that manages to be full of routine, at the same time as being full of flexibility and adaptations to observed behaviours.

Before anything else, dozens of humane cable restraints are placed at regular intervals on the tracks for the foxes, with the noose hanging loosely at head height, so that the passing fox is held still and uninjured until a keeper comes in the morning to shoot it. With modern restraints that do not tighten or strangle, quite often the fox is actually asleep when the keeper arrives, which they are required by law to do at least once a day. These restraints are designed to allow any untargeted animals – say, badgers or deer – to break out of them and continue on their way.

Predator Control: Late Spring

The tunnel traps, which were all disengaged at the end of the previous summer, but left in situ so that they maintain the smell and feel of the natural world, are re-landscaped, cleaned and reset. These traps are mainly for the inquisitive mustelids (stoats and weasels), but they will occasionally kill a rat that has allowed its appetite to overcome its natural caution and fear of anything new. Care is taken, as it has to be, to ensure that the entrance into the trap is too small to allow, say, a rabbit or a hedgehog to pass into it. With 750 of these traps, each taking around ten minutes to reactivate at the start of the season, it is hardly surprising that Charlie reckons that three-quarters of the entire workload for him and the team over the next six months will be predator control, especially taking into account everything else that has to be done. He is sanguine about the overall effect these traps have on the wildlife, pointing out that a weasel, which may only eat a couple of partridge chicks a year, will still be a relentless hunter-down of skylarks, yellowhammers, lapwings and other ground-nesting birds. He is adamant that the control work they do is why the bird counts and varieties are so strong here, year after year.

'Quite often, the best place for a cable restraint is right by a rabbit hole,' says Charlie. 'Most things that would eat a partridge would also eat a rabbit, given half a chance.'

Shooting, which can be an effective way of controlling rats and foxes, generally takes place at night because most ground predators operate more in the dark than in the day, a process greatly helped by the fact that the modern keeper can be equipped with night-viewing aids. At Peppering the four beat keepers are each expected to kill 200 rats a month, every month, a figure that is generally achieved, but which Charlie coincidentally believes hardly puts a dent in the population in a 'good' rat year. Like most environmentalists, he prefers not to use poison if at all possible, as there is always a small chance that a dead rat thus affected would work its way into and up the food chain, with devastating consequences. If he does use it, it is as mildly and effectively as possible, and he funnels the poison deep and vertically down into existing burrows that no other animal is going to enter, and from which no poisoned rat is going to emerge and head far.

'We know instantly when the poison has taken effect,' he says. 'The rats' droppings around the holes are blue. As soon as we see that, we make sure that we pick up any casualties as soon as we find them and incinerate them, out of harm's way.'

Avoiding poison is largely enabled by the keepers being able to see the large white heat-signature of the rat at night-time through the thermal-imaging devices with which they are equipped. An hour's evening walk down the lines of hedgerows and among the grain hoppers will often result in thirty or forty kills, night after night, made easier by the extraordinary steadiness under fire of *Rattus norvegicus*, which will often continue feeding regardless, when the animal next door has been shot and is lying on its back with its feet in the air. Rats have not gained their powerful foothold on the hinterland of the human ecosystem by being sentimental or jumpy.

'These devices cost a fortune,' says Charlie, 'but they are worth their weight in gold. If we didn't keep on top of the rats, especially in the period leading up to nesting, it is highly likely we wouldn't raise a single chick. We know that their bodies might attract in more raptors, such as buzzards and kites, who might in turn predate a few partridge chicks, but their impact is dwarfed by the potential impact of the rat.'

With corvids, control is generally achieved by use of a Larsen trap[7] during the breeding season, whereby a 'foreign' bird calls an inquisitive or aggressive local down into the trap

Predator Control: Late Spring

so as to check out the opposition. Alternatively, crows can be attracted into an area by use of a decoy or some pegged-out carrion and then shot.

The Peppering keepers operate in an area that is crisscrossed with footpaths and are therefore careful to do the majority of the control where it is not likely to cause upset to members of the general public.

'Having said that,' says Charlie, 'we will always explain what we are doing and, more importantly, why, when we are asked by a passing walker, for example, about a tunnel trap we are resetting. Ninety-nine times out of a hundred, the people we are talking to understand fully why we are doing it and what the benefits are. This is especially so with birdwatchers, who are suddenly able to grasp why their walk has been punctuated by the corn buntings, yellowhammers, skylarks and lapwings that they never seem to see anywhere else. Obviously not everyone is going to like the idea of killing one species to enable the survival of another, and we accept that.' Long gone are the days of the gamekeeper's gibbet standing in Gothic starkness against the skyline. Nowadays there is an instinctive understanding that predator control is not to everyone's taste, and that even those who understand and support it may not appreciate knowing too much about it.

The beat keepers are out at dawn, at dusk and often at all hours in between. You can hear their quad-bikes or buggies heading out of Charlie's yard to their own patches, as you might have heard them creep back in four or five hours before, from midnight lamping. These days theirs is work that stands in stark contrast to the nine-to-five indoor, highly connected lives of so many of their peers, but that is why they chose it. Each may have 150 traps and numerous restraints to check on his round, vegetation to clear, earth to smooth out, and water and feed for the crows in the Larsen traps. Later on in the summer, when the vegetation starts growing apace, they will need to spray off the tramlines to keep them open for passing traffic, and they have precious nests to check up on as they go. They work together and they work apart, exchanging news as they pass each other on the tracks to and from their beats, and sometimes sitting out in the night-watches waiting for a particularly crafty fox.

The task of predator control necessarily takes place alongside the routine work of housekeeping around the place – a job that includes putting up nest boxes for songbirds in the copses, open-fronted boxes for flycatchers and large-owl boxes on the edges of the woods. Hedges need to be pruned or laid, trees coppiced, gates repaired, feeding hoppers reconditioned and fences maintained. For people visiting for the first time and not intimately involved in the day-to-day workings of the estate, it can sometimes seem strange that so much effort is being put into supporting some species, while an equivalent amount is going into controlling another. But it is no more than a symptom of the effect that our Anthropocene era has had on the once-robust ecosystems that surround us.

By our relentless need to control and diminish the natural world around us, we are now obliged to take steps to protect those species whose fragility we have cruelly exposed.

If we don't, they go – and probably for ever.

8

THE SCIENTISTS: EARLY SUMMER

In any professional football season, each team starts with zero points. That is the baseline against which everything that happens to them – good or bad – in the next eight or nine months will be judged.

Likewise, estates that are involved in renaturing, or rewilding projects, generally seek a baseline figure for their biodiversity at the starting point, from which they will then get scientific guidance as to what they have, what they should aspire to and the steps they will need to take to make it happen. Where farm 'clusters' have come together, this process might involve as many as twenty farms, all working off the same information and guidance, and it can be a really useful, landscape-scale boost to the nature of the wider area. Many conservationists hope that one day the whole land will be covered by such clusters.

In the early days of the Peppering Project these surveys were done by Dick Potts in his capacity as a general ecologist, and his brief but informative reports then circulated around the key staff, with its recommendations forming the backbone of the coming year's work. By observing and analysing the presence and behaviour of the flora and fauna, sometimes with the help of local experts, Dick would come up with a logical plan of action for each problem or opportunity that he saw. This meant

The Return of the Grey Partridge

that the whole project was driven by observation and science, rather than caprice and fashion.

Dick would still be doing this work now in all probability but, following a cancer diagnosis at the beginning of 2017, he died on 30 March the same year, aged seventy-seven. While his lasting influence has spread far beyond the fields and partridges of Peppering, there is little doubt that he regarded what he had achieved there as the pinnacle of his professional life. In the *Guardian*'s obituary[1] Dick was described as having done 'more to bridge the gap between conservationists, farmers and the game-shooting fraternity than any other figure. He combined his training as a scientist, his background as a farmer's son and his passion for birds to help save the threatened grey partridge.' Through the groundwork laid down by his Sussex Study (still the longest-established survey of farmland ecosystems in Europe), he 'inspired a generation of scientists and led to new methods of conserving farmland birds'. The Game & Wildlife Conservation Trust (GWCT), of which he had once been director-general, highlighted the fact that his dry-sounding 'Studies on the Cereal Ecosystems' single-handedly pioneered conservation thinking outside pristine habitats, as opposed to those worked by man to produce food, fuel or fibre. 'It became', the GWCT said, 'the inspiration of a generation of ecologists who went on to amass a huge body of work.' Dick's monologue on grey partridges is still the authority on the species twenty-five years later, and a thousand of those conservation headlands and beetle banks that he helped to devise bloom around Britain each season, standing in testament to his forward thinking.

One of the eulogies at his memorial service was given, to no one's surprise, by Peter Knight. He concluded by pointing out that the day Dick died had been the same day 'as we found our

The Scientists: Early Summer

first lapwing nest of the season. I can now report that the four chicks hatched off. What Dick leaves behind is not something that is engraved in stone monuments, but something that is woven into the lives of others.' A total of £14,574 was collected at and around the funeral, to support the next generation of ecologists.

His widow, Olga, remembers Dick's early and lifelong aversion to chemicals, caused, she thinks, by watching shepherds drinking milk to protect themselves against the effects of the sheep dip they were using on his family farm, as a boy. She talks of how he was influenced by his work on seabirds as a young student, and how he came to link the unusual softness of the cormorants' eggs to the run-off of DDT from the fields above. She also highlights, above all things, Dick's optimism. 'Give nature a chance,' she recalls him saying on countless occasions, 'and nature will come through.'

Talking to his former colleagues on the estate, it is clear that while Dick's sudden death came as a hammer-blow to one and all, not least because they regarded him as a friend every bit as much as an adviser, they were fully aware that the only proper way to honour his memory was to get on with the job he had started, and to take it to even greater heights. Dick was not the type to go in for protracted 'goodbyes'.

In terms of the science, this meant getting in a new team of '-ologists' to follow up the surveys that he had started, and to build on the baseline he had created.

Conservation and ecology have many specialists, from herpetologists to mycologists through to ichthyologists and lepidopterists,[2] but the available time and budget suggested to Peter and Charlie that they concentrate on three key areas: plants, invertebrates and birds. That way, there would be a logical pyramid of action leading from the soil through the plants, the invertebrates and up to the birds, one of which happened to be the grey partridge.

'If the partridge is doing well,' says Charlie, 'then everything else is doing well. Projects like this need a driver and, even if it makes some people uncomfortable, providing a harvestable surplus of grey partridges is the driver round here. The potential income that they can generate for us will pay for the whole operation, which, in turn, will guarantee future biodiversity gains right across the estate, including the people who walk along its footpaths. So I ask the botanist a very simple question at the beginning of a season: how do we achieve a higher biomass of insects over the estate?'

Colin Hedley, the botanist in question, then makes a number of visits to the estate during the growing season and carries out what is, in effect, a wild-flower census over specific field borders, from which an annual report is compiled. Categorising what he sees into one of five groups (dominant, abundant, frequent, occasional and rare), he slowly draws his own professional conclusions about the effects of previous management, and his recommendations for the future. Criss-crossing the headlands, he sees not only the field pansies, sun spurge and henbit dead-nettles that are growing in the margins, but also, in his mind's eye, what lies beneath in the seed bank, waiting for disturbance to bring it once again into bloom. He points happily to the fumitory, knowing that it is a favourite of the turtle dove, a bird that the team would dearly like to entice back to Peppering; and notes the narrow-fruited cornsalad, a tiny plant that at least three generations of botanists before him would probably never have seen up here. He knows how important this is, and how the GWCT, on seeing the 2018 report on arable plants, told him that the Peppering Estate was now of national importance for arable flora.

The Scientists: Early Summer

'These days,' Colin points out, 'all the seed that is sold is cleaned beforehand, which removes one of the biggest drivers of wild-flower growth. So what happens on these headlands is incredibly important to the biodiversity of the whole farm. Sometimes, for example, I will suggest that they go against their general policy of minimum tillage, and actually plough an area or two to produce the disturbance that a lot of these wild flowers need to rise up out of the seed bank.'

On he walks, carefully noting everything down as he goes: thyme-leaved sandwort ('won't cope with any competition'), small toadflax ('ditto'), dwarf spurge ('high up on the Plantlife scoring system') and black medic ('the bully boy of the margins'), slowly creating a detailed wild-flower map of the ground that will inform future decisions downstream, will lead to more insects and then, eventually, to more ground-nesting birds. In all, he notes down twenty-four arable plant species for the day, of which eleven are what he terms 'important'.

Botanists tend to do field visits in the warmth of the afternoon, as opposed to entomologists (mid-morning, when the sun has dried the vegetation of its dew) or ornithologists (dawn, when the birds are most active), and it is getting late when Colin suddenly calls out. 'Come and look. Come and look!'

There is an almost childlike excitement on his face, and he points out a single rough poppy, the first time he has ever seen this vanishingly rare chalkland flower at Peppering. It has probably grown as a result of some disturbance, but it doesn't really matter.

It is here now, a beneficiary of twenty years of sympathetic stewardship, and will almost certainly increase over the coming years. And that is what counts.

A week later and in a neighbouring field, entomologist Graeme

Lyons is crouched over a large square tray, identifying invertebrates that he has just swept out of the same flowers Colin recently walked through. It is one of eight fields that have been chosen to represent a sample of size and management, and it closely mirrors what was used the previous year.

'What I see on the day obviously reflects the weather from the last few days,' he says, pointing out the lack of some of the scarcer short-grass species during the current damp summer. In each field he uses a mix of methods to ensure that he misses as little as possible: sweeping, suction-sampling (through an adapted hand-vacuum cleaner), grubbing and simply searching the flowers and the bare ground below. The silence of the fields is broken by the list that he softly describes and then notes down in his book.

'Wrinkled snail, ant damsel bug, forget-me-not shield bug, ruddy carpet moth, spindle ermine,' he says, but in Latin. 'Look! Here's a *Liparus coronatus*, nationally rare, and a *Chrysolina oricalcia* right next door. That's incredible.'

By the time Graeme's three visits (May, June and late July 2021) have been completed, he will have identified no fewer than 428 species, up by eighteen on the previous year, more than 8 per cent of which have local or national conservation status; 140 of these species alone are beetles, but he also notes the increase in bees, wasps and ants, including four particularly rare ones and the vulnerable *Andrena niveata*, which is thought to be a first for West Sussex. Taken as a two-year block of results with 2021 (to even out the specific conditions of either summer), he has recorded a total of 558 species on the estate,[3] with 10 per cent of them enjoying conservation status and a few nationally or locally rare.

'That's significantly higher than any of the individual years, and it's significantly higher than my rolling average. Meaning that this place is alive with invertebrates, far more than I would expect to see on normally managed downland. But, then, this isn't normally managed. It's one of the most bountiful areas that I will work on this year. Ever, in fact.' He clearly loves working these margins, just as Colin does.

Like most entomologists, Graeme will use the summer months for relentless field work and then the winter months to write it all up. The recommendations in the report that he will eventually produce, and which will run to a full forty-one pages of charts and tables, will form much of the basis of what Charlie and Conor will agree to plant, by way of cover crops and conservation headlands, for the following years. This time round, for example, he wants to see some more permanent grassland alongside the conservation headlands, so as to build up 'the reservoir of invertebrate diversity'.

'Working like this,' he says, as he packs up his equipment in the slanting sun after the long day, 'I continually find myself challenging scientific misconceptions, especially the binary and eye-catching headlines that shout out from social media about insect numbers, many of which have little or no basis in science.' As an example, he cites some evidence that, far from declining, some thermophilic[4] pollinator species are handling climate change well, even finding that it suits them.

'If everywhere was like this ...' he muses quietly, but doesn't need to finish the sentence.

The following Saturday, dawn hasn't even broken in the eastern sky when ornithologist Rich Black locks up his car in the Home Farm yard and begins the first of the eight individual kilometre-long transects that he will cover. He doesn't yet know what flowers Colin has found, or which invertebrates Graeme has unearthed during his own researches. Arable chalkland is his favourite habitat, and the weeds that it hosts are his favoured vegetation.

'Imagine', he suggests, 'a one-hundred-metre strip running for a kilometre. The aim is to identify and record as many of the birds that are in it as possible, divided into those within twenty-five metres, those out to a hundred metres, those beyond a hundred and those simply flying over.'

As he makes his slow way northwards, the early-summer dawn is alive with the movement and sound of its birdlife: wrens, whitethroats, goldfinches and mistle thrushes up on the high hedgerows. To his left linnets are rebuilding their nests and out there, way over on the hill to his right, he can distinctly make out the 'jangling keys' call of the now Red-Listed corn bunting, another direct beneficiary of the policy of farming for nature. 'Just over a hundred metres,' he concludes. Raven territories are increasing in number every year at Peppering, as elsewhere in the south-east, and the first pair of his day flaps massively across the sky above and in front of him. 'Overfly,' he writes. Woodpigeons, whose granivorous lifestyle has enabled them to treble in numbers in recent years right across the country, explode out of the tops of hedges as he passes, wings clapping.

Raptor numbers (owls included) have prospered over the last two decades, and it would be an unfortunate walker who didn't spot hen and marsh harriers, sparrowhawks, peregrines and even the occasional goshawk. Rich notes how the population of buzzards has slowly declined in direct contrast to the explosion of red kites, and how ash dieback disease, normally so damaging to the ecology of the woodlands, has actually been beneficial to the woodpecker. In nature, nothing is simple, and everything is connected. Peppering may be an oasis of biodiversity, but it can never be immune to the prevailing national and regional trends.

The Scientists: Early Summer

As it happens, Rich isn't the only bird specialist on the farm this morning. High up among the broken lines of the spring cultivations, PhD student Ryan Burrell is checking the static cameras that he has sited on the lapwing nests to see who, or what, has been sniffing around in the night. Lapwings, besides being yet another Red-Listed bird in an increasingly lengthy British catalogue,[5] are highly effective at indicating information about the general quality of the habitat. The lapwing's survival strategy on a nest that, at first glimpse, seems to be almost ridiculously exposed is to use that very exposure to spot trouble coming early, and then to take evasive and distracting action on behalf of the eggs below. This has worked well in recent years, and no fewer than thirty broods will fledge this year, up from nineteen the year before. Ryan well understands the dividend that the Red-Listed lapwings earn from the predator control that goes on all around them, just as he knows that this tiny, thriving island population is a highly vulnerable drop in the surrounding ocean of swathes of countryside where they no longer breed at all.

Statistically, Rich has picked up where Dick Potts left off and is able to report continual increase in the abundance of a wide variety of Red-Listed species over and above the lapwings and grey partridges. Skylark pairs have more than doubled in five years, for example, as have linnets and most raptors and owls. This is in stark contrast to the national figures, which have shown a miserable decline of 57 per cent in farmland birds since 1970, and an even more dramatic 80 per cent reduction in grey partridges and corn buntings over the same period. And it is this abundance, rather than variety, that continually impresses the ecologists, for variety can sometimes be a matter of luck, but abundance can't. Moreover, with abundance comes a small measure of security against, say, a wet breeding season

The Return of the Grey Partridge

or a brutally cold winter. As in most conservation projects, the long-term aim is for some level of equilibrium.

This particular year, Rich has two recommendations on his mind. First, he would like to see still more hedgerows, and some of them to include curved rather than straight edges, so as to create little microclimates of sheltered space and warmth for the local breeders. Second, he will ask for the contractor to turn off the seed drill from time to time as he is sowing later in the year, so that skylark plots can be enhanced and second broods encouraged.

'It really is that granular,' he says.

Which is good because, in the early days at least, attention to detail is king in the grand plan to allow nature to surge back into the landscape.

When the nights are drawing in and the clocks have gone back, everyone meets up in the estate office for a round-table discussion of what has been found, and what the various farming and stewardship implications are.

No one present – not farmer, gamekeeper, ecologist, manager or even duke – looks entirely at home out of the fields and back in the office environment, but the two hours they spend together will be the engine room for future land management, so they are all keen to be there and happy to hear what is going on outside their own area of interest. Because each specialist works on a number of other farms and estates, both locally and nationally, the meeting is also an informal opportunity to benchmark their own progress and performance.

'Besides,' someone says, 'it's nice to see how we are getting on alongside the others. Just because it's nature doesn't mean it can't be a bit competitive.'

Anyway, it is all to nature's benefit if the others are gaining

The Scientists: Early Summer

species too, and the conservation network is always alive with stories of success – and failure – from around the country, from which lessons can profitably be learned. Up in North Norfolk, at Holkham (admittedly a different habitat to these chalky downs), a changed management regime for the wetland fields has led to huge and quick increases in lapwing, redshank and spoonbill, as you might expect, as well as reed bunting. And it's not always straightforward. In fact it's not ever straightforward. For example, more otters sometimes mean less riverine birdlife, at least for a time; famously, the huge plus of DDT being banned, following the publication of Rachel Carson's *Silent Spring* in 1962, led to a bounce in the sparrowhawk population that went on to decimate Britain's bullfinches, and possibly therefore a stay of execution for many a budding apple tree (the bullfinch eats the buds). The secret in dealing with the complex connectivity of nature, if there is one, is really no more than to keep your eyes wide open and learn from what you see.

The afternoon wears on. The team talks of thickening the hedges, and allowing them wavy lines both in the vertical and horizontal dimensions, which affects Conor, as it will be more time-consuming to work farm machinery around them, but will benefit finches; of setting out a series of one-metre-wide ponds alongside some of the hedges, primarily to help the partridges, but also to provide an attractive habitat for the Red-Listed turtle dove, which needs the water it provides for the crop milk she needs for her chicks; they discuss how to thicken cover to bring in nightingales, and an experimental approach to the 'plough versus no-plough' debate. Rich talks about radio-tracking surprises, such as hen grey partridges for some reason leading their chicks into the middle of sprayed fields where there can be no possible food for them.

Areas of genuinely conflicting interests are embraced,

not avoided, such as the potential effect of the new inversion ploughing on insect numbers, and the demands that Red Tractor certification[6] makes, regarding the cleanliness and tidiness of farmyards. Tidiness, as every country person knows, is the enemy of biodiversity. Likewise, dropping seed rates is all very well for Graeme's insect numbers, but Colin knows that the resulting space created can quickly get infested by bully-boy weeds like black medic.

In many ways, all this is about creating habitats to order, salting the mine for target species such as cornflowers, pheasant's eyes, dingy skipper butterflies and those elusive turtle doves, and making sure that no earlier gain is lost through oversight. But they all support the idea that these things must be done slowly, incrementally and, if possible, measured against controls. This project is all about variety and, as far as possible, mimicking nature.

'Doing everything all at once is the downfall of modern farming,' points out Eddie, to general agreement. 'Obsessing about biomass simply leads to factory farming.'

Bit by bit, the component parts of the conversation become like little rivulets that feed into larger streams, which finally flow into the river of next year's plan. Conor will then look at the implications on his yields and stewardship schemes, and will work with Sue over the winter to create a financial plan that both supports the biodiversity aims and satisfies the estate's trustees. Charlie will think about the siting of the new ponds, the composition of the new cover crops and headlands, and the implications on the partridge drives and the workload of his beat keepers.

One by one, the ecologists make their goodbyes and head off for their cars, and the next project.

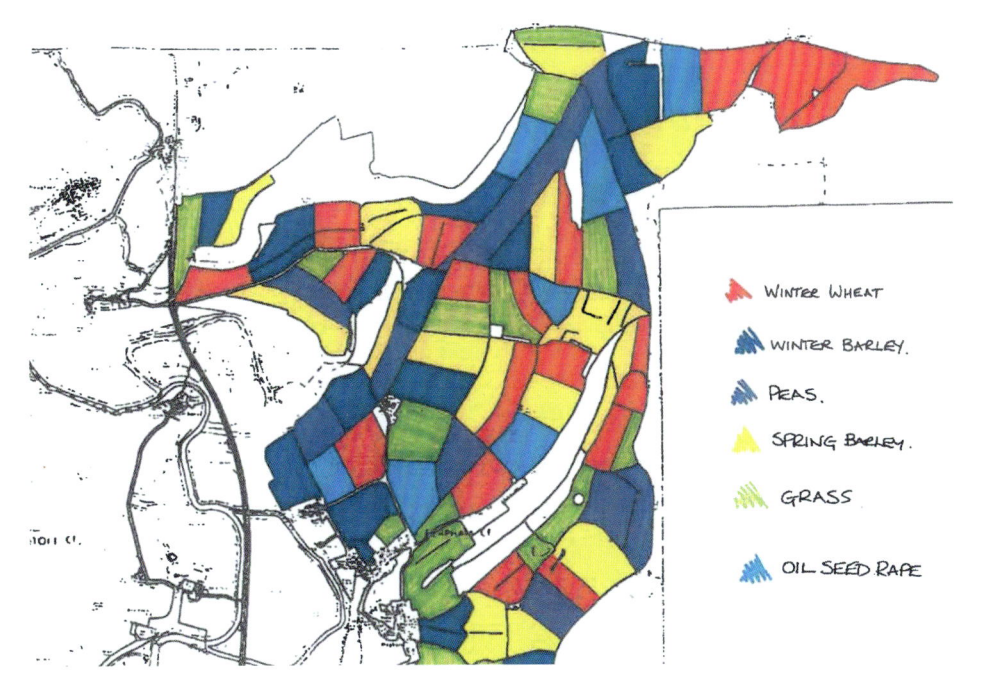

Farming system changed from block farming to multi-crop 'patchwork quilt' approach.

Post-2002, a patchwork of different crops and hedgerows.

Land sharing: a conservation headland for restoring wild arable flowers, with normal arable for food production beyond.

New hedges are planted on top of newly created beetle banks.

Hedges are laid on a rotational basis to maximise cover at the base.

Back after a gap of maybe 50 years, a rough poppy.

From two pairs to a thousand, the grey partridge was always the driver of the renaturing.

A successful conclusion to a clutch reared only feet from a footpath.

The rapid increase in small mammals has seen an equally rapid increase in owls; here, the short-eared variety.

A hen harrier flies over the low ground with Arundel Castle in the background.

Bio-abundance in action: linnets and a couple of goldfinch explode from a hedge.

Over 1,000 hares regularly patrol the fields and margins of Peppering.

The margins have created a perfect habitat for butterflies; here, a common blue.

These days the jangling keys call of the Red-Listed corn bunting is heard throughout the farm.

Crucial chick food: *Stenotus binotalus*.

Both urban and rural foxes frequent Peppering. Consequently ground-nesting birds need protection through legal predator control.

Predator control is strictly regulated, with humane best practice observed, for example, through this Tully trap.

Modern restrainers restrain foxes, which can later be dispatched. The restrainers do not affect badger or deer.

The Red-Listed lapwing has benefited directly from the new management system.

All head-started curlews were ringed; a dozen had GPS attached to them so that their movements could be monitored once they had flown.

Charlie Mellor (foreground) and Graeme Lyons checking insect numbers during high summer.

Driving grey partridges is a highly skilled practice that had to be learned again once shooting re-started.

The shoot is the heart of the team's work. Sometimes numbers will permit only one day a season.

Wild grey partridges star-burst over the hedge as soon as they see a line of guns, making them a highly challenging quarry.

The picking-up team at the end of a successful day.

The Duke of Norfolk (left) and Dick Potts, 2007.

9

CURLEWS: HIGH SUMMER

In May the curlews came.

They didn't come in from the coast, as potential breeding pairs flying their musical way to the hills from Pagham Harbour or the tidal muds of Bosham; neither were they late arrivals from the North Sea flats of Holland or from the marshes of France. Instead they came to Peppering in the back of a Land Rover Discovery, after a 320-mile drive south from the moors of Arkengarthdale in North Yorkshire. There were forty eggs in five mobile incubators, part of an experiment to see if the habitat and land-management processes that had been in place for two decades could make a suitable enclave for nationally threatened curlews to breed once again.[1]

Even saying 'once again' is a debatable point. There are no hard-and-fast records of the Eurasian curlew breeding on the South Downs, although it is almost certain they once did. After all, much of the habitat would have been close to perfect for them before the dawn of industrial farming. But two decades into the new millennium, with curlew numbers in Britain having declined by around 70 per cent in fifty years,[2] there seemed to be little point in worrying about the finer details.

In global terms, only Russia and Finland support larger breeding populations than Britain, so there is a growing national responsibility to protect them. They may be but one bird of the more than 200 that regularly breed in Britain, but they are also an indicator species, speaking out eloquently for other ground-nesting birds, such as the lapwing, yellowhammer or skylark, and via them for the general health of the country's grassland and farmland. With their bubbling call and charismatic looks, curlews could also be said to speak out eloquently for a generation of declining nature. Estates like Peppering have the ability and resources to play their part in the national revival of an iconic bird, and Eddie was not prepared to pass it up. Indeed, he increasingly felt it to be an obligation, no matter what obstacles were thrown in his way. After all, the generally accepted figure was that Britain needs to produce 10,000 *extra* curlew chicks a year to avoid eventual extinction, against which the Peppering forty would be a mere drop in the ocean. But the exercise would pay for itself overnight if, two years later, when those freshly released curlews were old enough to breed, they came back to Peppering to do so. That would open up opportunities in a hundred different locations elsewhere, some of which were already lining up to volunteer their services.

'The crashing populations in nature aren't going to be rescued by endless scoping papers, five-year studies and eighty-five-page procedural documents,' Eddie told the team. 'They'll be saved by people like us getting off their backsides now and acting immediately. If we can get the call of the curlew up above the South Downs, maybe we can also have an impact locally and inspire the people who live round here.' In saying this, he was perhaps also subconsciously articulating a general frustration with the lack of speed and urgency behind much of British conservation, in which cautious scientists would take months, and often years, to recognise what the field workers could see every time they left their own front doors, and where the answer to most given problems seemed to be to set in train yet another study. If the last twenty years on the farm had proved anything at all, it had shown that biodiversity decline could be halted, and reversed, far more quickly than was widely thought.

'We just don't have time for that old approach any more,' Eddie repeated over and over again, and to anyone who would listen. 'The disappearance of the curlew is happening right now and needs immediate action.'

By the end of that first curlew summer, more than £40,000 (or more than £1,000 a bird) had been spent by the estate on the new project, 3.1 kilos of paperwork generated in order to gain the appropriate licences to go ahead and thousands of hours of extra work undertaken. If it all seemed to be an enormous additional effort for a workforce who were already busy, it unashamedly was. Eddie's own view was that, as a metaphor for the healing of the British countryside, the curlew was possibly the only bird that spoke more loudly than even the grey partridge.

'And it's not even a game bird,' agreed Charlie. 'So it might help people to understand that we don't just do this stuff, and spend this money, so that people can shoot. There's so much more to it than that.' In saying this, he also knew that the estate was in the privileged position of already having in its team of beat keepers an effective habitat and predator-management regime that would could actively support the project from day one. In fact, as much as anything, that was why they had been able to secure the licences in the first place.

Besides, with all the conservation and third-way farming work that had been carried out over the last twenty years, what Peppering had to offer *Numenius arquata* could almost have been scripted by the bird itself.

The practice of head-starting – as the process of translocating fertile eggs from areas of abundance to areas of shortage is known – is a complex and sometimes controversial activity. Like surgery, it is something to be done only when the only other options are a continued decline towards local or national extinction. Because while it undeniably puts healthy birds into the air where they are currently absent, it will only ever be a sticking-plaster solution against the need for landscape-scale habitat management. If the landscape remains unfriendly and the predation out of control, the birds will either not come back to breed or, if they do, will fail.

In theory, it is simple. Whole clutches of newly laid eggs are taken from birds (which should then go on again to replace them with a second clutch), incubated mechanically in their new home and then raised in the safety of a large run, while they grow and get used to a parentless life in a new place. All head-started birds are ringed, and a good proportion will be fitted with satellite tags that will subsequently feed back important information about where they go over the coming seasons and, where – if anywhere – they breed. Then, at the age when that species of bird would naturally fledge and make its own way in the world, they are released. There is previous information available, but it tends to relate to other breeds, which might behave entirely differently under the same circumstances. Project Godwit, for example, an initiative to help increase the black-tailed godwit population in the Ouse Washes, has seen the pair count rise from three in 2017 to nineteen in 2021, which is hugely encouraging. But curlews are not godwits, and it will only be well after this book is published that the team will know whether they have been successful.

Then again, this was really no more complicated than what had been gifted by the Duke of Edinburgh all those years ago, when he sent Eddie that 'parcel' of nine pairs of Sandringham grey partridges to seed the revival of the Peppering population.

However, since then the process had become a lot more bureaucratic and needed a great deal more formal paperwork and process.

The idea of moving curlew eggs from his grouse moor at Arkengarthdale in Yorkshire, where the birds were still thriving, to Peppering had first come to the Duke as a serious proposition in the summer of 2020.

At first he was given a rude awakening into the legal realities of head-starting by Nigel Winter, the Arkengarthdale head keeper, who drily replied to the request to send some eggs down south with the immortal comeback, 'So long as you're happy for me to spend a year or two in jail, your grace.'[3] From that point, and now understanding the legal framework involved, the team worked hard for six months to prepare their application for the licence from Natural England that they would need in order to move the eggs. Part of this was to demonstrate that the habitat and habitat management at Peppering were commensurate with the risk of the project failing, but a significant part was also to show that the Yorkshire curlews — the donors — wouldn't suffer as a result. With eggs taken early enough, the female will lay a second clutch, but the guidance as to which estate, and which part of that estate, the chicks would come from was detailed and not always straightforward. By and large, clutches that were considered already vulnerable were selected, such as those very close to footpaths, or those in the middle of fields from which silage would be cut. The fact that Arkengarthdale had more than doubled its breeding curlew pairs between 2007 (when there were sixty pairs) and 2021 (by which time this had increased to 134) was critical to the whole project, as was Eddie's willingness to pay for it out of his own pocket. Among the three kilos of paperwork that led to the issue of the licences was a series of maps that set out the precise location of each one of the 134 nests – the result of intense observation by the keepers at Arkengarthdale and of local volunteers.

By 7 March 2022 the application was formally submitted, and by early May it had received approval. This delay had injected huge urgency into the move of the eggs, both on the basis of needing to collect them early enough so that they were replaced, and so that there was no risk of them hatching before, or during, the transit journey. On 16 May, having established that Eddie's Land Rover Discovery would afford the smoothest ride of any vehicle on the estate, the forty eggs, sitting in five separate state-of-the-art incubators, left Arkengarthdale for the south. This was not a moment too soon, as the first egg was busy pipping[4] even as it made its way around the M25. By the time the incubators had been rigged up in Charlie's state-of-the-art hatchery, the first head-starting curlew chick was actively breaking out of its shell, and others were lining up to follow.

Back at Peppering, frantic work had been taking place to create a curlew nursery in Charlie's yard. For the first week or so, the incubators (and subsequent hatchers) would merely need to be in a secure room with the relevant equipment, but once the birds were around a week old, they would require large purpose-built pens with complete protection from both ground and avian predators. Two adjacent pens, each forty metres by six, were built by the team of keepers and equipped with shelters, lamp heaters, feeders, water trays, nets on top, tunnel traps alongside, and six strands of electricity providing more than a slight shock to any forgetful worker going in to check on them.

Of the forty eggs that arrived, two turned out to be infertile and one didn't hatch, leaving thirty-seven. Of these, two of the chicks had a disorder known as 'wryneck', where the bird's neck seems to lack the strength to support the head in the early days; in the wild, these wouldn't have survived more than a day or so, but it was agreed to monitor their progress closely to see if they recovered sufficiently to be released. All the eggs hatched between 16 and 26 May and were subsequently allocated to one of two groups ('older' and 'younger'), which would eventually dictate where and when they were released.

In the early days, Charlie's job changed from head keeper to nursery maid to the new arrivals. His wife, Kate, was not immune either: from taking down the measurements and weights that Charlie shouted out three times a day, to creating little neck splints for the 'wrynecks', it was a full-time occupation, and one that had to be juggled between her own day job and the shared school runs. This came as no great surprise to Kate, who knew well and accepted the pivotal role of the head keeper's partner in enabling the various out-of-hours jobs to be done. In fact anyone turning up in the yard in the early days of June could easily have found themselves press-ganged into helping to candle suspect eggs, cleaning out bedding or assisting in the complex protocols of the daily routines. Even people researching for books on the Peppering adventure were found to have their uses, in the morning feeds and health checks.

Every egg had its own individual and clutch code, needed weighing on a daily basis and, after hatching, had its shell secured and sent back for scientific analysis. And this all had to be done under conditions of intense cleanliness, with boot dips and frequent deep-cleaning simply a fact of life. Almost as soon as the birds were hatched, they were ringed and then subject to a developing information chart that would make a human child's medical records look like shorthand in the extreme.

What was going on was at once stringently regulated by scientists and civil servants and utterly reliant on the centuries-old skills of career countrymen. Day by day, the chicks grew in the safety of their shed.

'Anyone with a basic knowledge of birds can rear a curlew' was Charlie's view, and he had been rearing birds since he was five years old. 'In fact their innate wildness makes them much easier than pheasants or red-legged partridges. Even when we had a violent summer thunderstorm one evening, which would have killed quite a proportion of pheasants, the curlews just found shelter and got on with it.'

By early June, Charlie was starting to move the birds into the outdoor rearing pens, which – although it still involved multiple visits each day for feeding, watering and monitoring purposes – was not quite so time-consuming as the early days. There was a certain amount of interest from local raptors overflying the pens, but not as much as had been feared and, in the end, it was pretty short-lived.

In the outdoor pens it was a question of starting the curlews off in the little shelter and then giving them an increasingly large area to walk around and stretch their wings, increasing the feed and the water-tray size, and soaking part of the ground so that they could let those long bills do what they instinctively knew they should be doing, which was probing for worms. Twice a day they underwent a mobile health check – fundamentally no more than a march past, whereby Charlie could review their general health, how they were walking and whether or not they were starting to carry any physical problems. For one of these problems, known as 'angel wings' or 'slipped wings', which is thought to be caused by too high a proportion of protein in the pellets, the immediate solution was to tape the affected bird's wing up and monitor how it got on. This was all fine, but it had to be done with the minimum of human–curlew togetherness, so that the birds did not develop a dangerous lack of fear of *Homo sapiens*.

Day by day the curlews grew larger, as their iconic bills lengthened and started their classic de-curving. And day by day they became more aware of their surroundings, and more interested in extending their great wings and flying around to the maximum extent that the construction of the cage allowed. Individual characters developed – some feisty, some cautious, some adventurous – and the occasional noisy but harmless spat would break out from time to time over the feeding trays, maybe indicating the healthy restlessness that accompanies a young bird's approaching fledging.

Two days before their release, fifteen selected birds were fitted with tiny satellite tags that would enable their progress to be tracked, wherever they went, once they had been released. While, on one plane, this project was just a routine, if time-consuming exercise in the husbandry of rearing birds, on the other plane, it was an adventure deep into the cutting edge of science, where the results (whatever they were) would directly add to the body of information that would then go on to inform the wider debate. No one on the team, or even among the scientific advisers at GWCT, could say with any assurance whether the birds would eventually come back 'home', go south to France, east to the Baltic or even 300 miles north to Arkengarthdale. Previous generations of satellite trackers stopped working once the battery ran out, but the ones used for the Peppering curlews had tiny solar-charging panels on them, raised up so that the feathers would not eventually be preened back into place over the top. After all this activity, one thing the team did know: those tiny trackers, each one worth around £1,200, would be sharing the birds' most private moments from the minute they took to the Sussex skies. (Six months later, those private moments have been revealed as taking place mainly along the south coast of England, as far west as the Scilly Isles, but predominantly in the estuaries of the rivers Exe and Hamble and in the vastness of Poole Harbour. One bird appears to have made its home in a gravel pit near Gatwick Airport.)

The remaining birds were split into two further groups: those that would simply be radio-tagged, so that they could be followed on a local basis, and a control group that had neither radio nor satellite. This was a time-consuming process, as each bird, whatever its grouping, had to be caught, held, measured and weighed, before being taken out to the release site so that it would become habituated to the location once the doors were thrown open. It is forbidden to attach more than 3 per cent of a bird's body weight to it, in the way of rings and scientific equipment, so any bird below 550 grams automatically defaulted to the control group. Finally the birds were moved to a release pen that Charlie had sited a couple of miles away from the yard, in a situation that offered decent curlew habitat with a measure of privacy from footpaths.

A day later, on the evening of 13 July 2022, and only when the searing summer sun had lost some of its intensity, the doors of the release pen were quietly opened. For a second or two, nothing happened. Then, emboldened perhaps by the prospect of flying more than a couple of metres off the ground for a change, one female walked to the entrance, opened her wings and simply set off into the sultry air in the general direction of the coast. While she was turning round to complete a giant circle, the others came out after her, some trotting for the safety of the longer grass just up the hill and others taking to the air, calling all the while.

Curlews: High Summer

The whole team was down there for the release and, for a while, no one said anything at all. Nothing needed saying. Given the extent of the planning and the work, any emotion was an understandable reaction. And, in so many ways, it was a defining moment in the twenty-year-long journey that had preceded it. That it could even have been contemplated needed all the improvements and innovations that had taken place incrementally over that period. But that it had actually been done required a depth of ambition and commitment beyond what even Dick Potts would have expected.[5] Even so, there was a general understanding that this had been the easy bit. Regular information would come back from the satellite trackers from now on of course, but it would be at least two years before the arrival on the farm (or not) of a red-and-yellow tagged breeding curlew, calling out that bubbling song all the while, would start to prove that the whole exercise had been worth it.

'You know, I'm not really sure I ever fully believed that I'd hear that sound over the Downs in my lifetime,' said Eddie as they made their way back to the vehicles. 'It kind of makes me wonder what's next.'

'Corncrakes,' said Charlie. 'I think we can do corncrakes. Or red-backed shrikes,' he added as an afterthought.

A week later the evidence from the satellite trackers was that seven of the curlews were not only still on Peppering ground, but were also resting up in the same field of long grass. One had headed a dozen miles east to Brighton, and another the same distance west to Pagham. While they were now going to have to wait at least two years until the curlews were mature enough to come back to Peppering to breed (or not, as the case may be) a few months later the team got the other news they most wanted to hear.

Natural England – cautious from the outset of the project, on the basis of the lack of past breeding records from the area – had seen enough not only to extend the licensing to a full five years, but also to grow the headstarting initiative in size and scope. From 2023 onwards, this means that 120 eggs will come down from Arkengarthdale and Bolton Castle instead of forty, and they will be distributed evenly to three estates and not merely to one. From now on, Cranborne in Dorset and Elmley Nature Reserve in Kent will join Peppering at the curlew party.

This was not only significant from the conservation point of view, although that was reason enough to proceed. What it also meant was that, with four more years of visibility now achieved, commercial organisations could be approached for support in financing what was an extremely expensive project, as part of their environmental, social and governance work.

Right now, it had cost well over £1,000 to get each curlew into the air.

10

THE SOIL UNDERNEATH: LATE SUMMER

Once, before the curlews, there were mammoths here.

And because there were mammoths, and other megafauna[1] roaming the land, along with a whole suite of predators to control them, the ecosystems were normally in a healthy state of equilibrium. In short, energy was being 'transferred in a sustainable way between vegetation and animals via food webs',[2] such as predator and prey, in a process known scientifically as trophic cascade. The actions of the grazers and herbivores dictated the amount and type of vegetation, and the actions of the predators dictated the quantity of grazers. But since the Neolithic age, man has been sticking his Anthropocene oar in, creating unnatural clearings and applying stringent demands – not to mention chemicals – on a land and a biodiversity, which eventually rewarded him by altering beyond recognition and, in the case of the biodiversity, gradually disappearing. Furthermore, by restricting the ability of animals to roam freely around different habitats, mainly by fencing, and by stopping natural disturbances, such as fire, by taming the countryside, man utterly altered the ground around him. And not for the better.

By the mid-1990s a new thinking started to drift eastwards over the Atlantic from America, eventually becoming known as 'rewilding', under which the natural cycle of life would be allowed to re-establish itself in specific areas, by the controlled introduction of those old natural processes, by a lack of cultivation and with emphasis on the contribution of large herbivores. At its simplest, rewilding is probably no more than an answer to the question of 'So what?' to the scientific discovery of the causes behind the disappearance of the megafauna.

In Europe the first major appearance of rewilding was in a nature reserve outside Amsterdam called Oostvaardersplassen, where biodiversity has improved hugely, even if commuters on the adjacent motorway system are occasionally distressed by the sight of unfed livestock dying against the fence during harsh winters. Since then, rewilding has been passionately extended to a number of high-profile but highly localised estates around Britain, with some extraordinary success in reintroductions. In many parts of Europe, apex predators like wolves and lynx are sidling quietly back into the countryside of their own accord, but in Britain, which is both an island and highly risk-averse, this is not going to happen in the foreseeable future. And in default of an apex predator, the trophic cascade will never fully work.

Ironically, for a concept that is about nature reasserting itself, rewilding is in fact an extremely controlled form of land management, often micromanaged down to individual species level, and with outcomes that are closely monitored throughout every different activity. Also, being fashionable and widely misunderstood, it is subject to a variety of different interpretations, many of which amount to little more than shoving in an extra cover crop or two and a bit of hedge-planting. 'Why don't you try a bit of rewilding here?' a visitor suggested one evening at Peppering, under a sky full of larks and to the chorus of the rusty-gate calls of headlands full of grey partridge.

The Soil Underneath: Late Summer

'What had you got in mind?' answered Charlie, to a long silence. 'What else, exactly, do we need to do?'

So, from the start, Eddie and the team had no particular interest in following the rewilding approach. Their duty as farmers, as they saw it, was to feed the world, and their aim as conservationists was to show that food production could be done efficiently and effectively on this marginal land, with an abundance of nature filling every gap that wasn't actually being farmed. Not only that, but they believed this practice could then be followed in smaller farms with fewer resources. Specifically, the team also thought that it was only by creating thousands of linked corridors of biodiversity, out of dozens of similar farms and parks, that the crisis in Britain's biodiversity could start to be addressed properly. The land was hard, up there on the chalky side of the Downs, sure enough, but it was still capable of filling a bread basket under the right conditions, and of growing the raw material for beer and providing protein and wool from the carcasses and fleeces of sheep. More importantly, it was still capable of doing all this under a cloud of insects, and between a pattern of vibrant hedges.

They called it 'the third way', but they could equally have called it 'renaturing'. You could go for a rewilding safari up the road, if you wanted, or you could walk through 1,500 hectares of renaturing, on any of the footpaths around Peppering.

But to make it count, they had first to understand how to get the hard land to work equally hard for them. Even more so as they had long ago devoted 15 per cent of it to nature's restoration. Restoring nature could do many things, but it couldn't improve the ground or raise the organic content of the soil, quickly or on its own.

*

It is one thing choosing between rewilding and renaturing, if, indeed, there is a real choice to be made, but quite another to create a soil quality that will not only support all that the farm is doing now, but will grow richer and better as time goes on. After all, the pyramid of life above, which includes plants, invertebrates and birds, can only thrive if the soil below is thriving itself. As the American broadcaster Paul Harvey once famously put it, 'Despite all our achievements, we owe our existence to a six-inch layer of topsoil and the fact that it rains'.

In effect, what this means is that in order to give maximum support to both the productivity of the farm and the return of its nature, the farming itself has to be regenerative. Fundamentally, this entails being handed over in due course to the next generation in a better condition than it had been found by the current one.

Like rewilding, regenerative farming is a term widely, and sometimes even deliberately, misunderstood. It shouldn't be. It is a set of simple principles, more than a code of hard-and-fast rules, and is for guidance rather than strict adherence. Those principles are to avoid disturbing the soil, to keep the soil surface covered at all times, to keep living roots in the soil, to grow a diverse range of crops and to involve grazing animals within the rotation.[3] And if those principles are followed diligently, the soil will improve in quality, in structure and in its percentage of organic matter. That, in turn, will improve the stability and drainage of the farm and, years later maybe, the quality of the water that drains away from it.

Chalky soil, like that at Peppering, is inherently low in organic matter, so Conor's work is cut out from the outset. Fundamentally what he needs to do is increase that matter in around 90 per cent of the farm's area, but leave it low in the remainder, which is grassland, suitable only for grazing sheep, not for growing crops. Where he is increasing it, he is aiming to get the organic-matter percentage up from a level of around 2–3 per cent to somewhere nearer 6–7 per cent by the end of the decade. Like everything else around here – the flowers, the insects and the birds – this is verifiable by science, year on year.

To achieve this, Conor has three main weapons at his disposal and, if he uses them well, he will also end up creating easier water retention, greater biodiversity and far less reliance on manufactured inputs.

First, he applies farmyard manure, and lots of it: more than 6,000 tonnes a year. The majority of it, about 5,000 tonnes, comes from a local pig unit, while the remainder is brought in from local cattle herds on a straight straw-for-dung swap: Conor's wheat or barley straw for someone else's manure. The financial equation on the pig manure is a relatively simple one too: £2 per tonne to buy it, £10 to transport it and £2 to spread it. At around 25 tonnes per hectare, this still produces an overall cost that is around half of what would otherwise have been spent on bought-in inputs. More importantly, though, the soil improvement will reap unseen financial benefits, such as increased trace elements and friability,[4] benefits that will also be incremental over the years, rather than just in the crop for one season. Every hectare is tested before the spring application, with the result that every application is no more than is required.

Second, he introduces 'green manure' that is the result of his cover-cropping plan – a plan that also ensures that no part of the ground is bare, even in the deepest winter. Green manure is the end product of the act of leaving the root systems of cover crops in the ground, once livestock have topped them off. At any one time 20 per cent of the farm will be under cover crop, which might be, say, mustard and radish to improve the soil before the sheep graze it off, and then the next crop – wheat or barley – is direct-drilled into the ground. Over the course of a full rotation, the sheep will be let loose to graze on almost all areas of the farm.

Finally, Conor also works to improve the soil fertility by adding bought-in compound fertiliser as and when he needs it, based on whatever the local crop of the moment happens to be. This is only ever meant to be a temporary crop-specific measure, helpful to the yield, but not necessarily to the long-term health of the soil from which it is springing. Being expensive, and in an age of soaring input costs, Conor will resort to this as seldom as he reasonably can.

With an informed mix of those three approaches, the raw materials should be in place for the farm to play its essential part in creating the income that will go on to support nature's bounty along its unfarmed corridors.

More importantly, that 'six-inch layer of topsoil' that Paul Harvey talked about will be steadily growing in quality and organic matter. Up here, this is a vital ingredient in just about all future plans.

Then there is the livestock.

The function of livestock at Peppering – alongside the important one of providing a return on investment at the end of their lives – is to improve the soil around the farm by manuring it (with their dung and urine) and aerating it (with their hooves). Essentially this is a choice between pigs, cattle, sheep, or a mixture of all three. Conor has worked with all three in the past and on other farms, but a herd of 1,600 Romney ewes is what he has inherited, so anything else that comes in needs to do so on the wings of a persuasive argument for change.

For the time being, he is avoiding pigs. While outdoor

pig-rearing (which is the type that he would do, if he had pigs) would be good for the soil for its ammonia content, the feeling is that this advantage would be outweighed by the sheer damage that pigs will do to the ground in a wet winter, and by the compaction that comes from their own weight and from the tyres of the tractor bringing daily feed out to them. Also, next to chickens, pigs are the livestock with the most reliance on outside food sources and, indirectly through that, use up vast acreages of land elsewhere to keep them fed. Pigs would also entail specialist staff, in addition to the two shepherds already employed.

The decision on cattle is more complex. Conor acknowledges the cow's central role as a biodiversity engineer and an improver of the ground, but the fact that there is no natural water around the farm means that it would all have to be transported; and the fact that there is no permanent fencing, save that employed to keep walkers' dogs out of the main partridge nesting areas, makes it a more complicated operation.

'We can have cattle whenever we want them,' he says, 'simply by providing grazing for the local herds that need it. Anyway, we get three tonnes of muck for every tonne of straw we send out, which slightly does the job that the cow would have done anyway.'

The real issue about having a permanent herd of cows on what is primarily a shooting estate has nothing to do with soil quality, though. If it was just down to that metric, the cow would probably be chosen every time. No, the main potential problem is more connected to the cow's general disposition to want to be wherever it currently isn't, and to use its weight and intelligence to break through any surrounding fencing so as to enable that. If sheep escape an enclosure, they are apt to stay quite close by and to inflict only minimal damage; if cows do it, they will likely plough up an entire cover crop overnight, knock over neighbouring feeders and probably rub themselves up against any available surface for good measure. On a farm this would be a mere occupational risk; on a sensitive shooting estate, especially one run at the behest of nature, it could be a complete disaster, especially if part of the collateral damage is the precious partridge nests.

So Peppering sticks with its Romney sheep, harvesting an ongoing and profitable protein source when the lambs are sent off to market from August onwards, and an annual haul of wool that, these days, doesn't cover even half the cost of bringing in the shearers who do the work. The flock is managed by two employed shepherds and, in addition to the permanent pasture that makes up perhaps 15 per cent of the farm, each bit of the remainder of the estate can expect a useful visit from them at least every eight years, according to the rotation plan. The sheep, that is, and not necessarily the shepherds.

Then it's just about the trees and the water.

The issue surrounding trees is relatively straightforward. They are a rare example of where the aims of the farm and those of the shoot can become mutually exclusive. From the farmer's point of view, additional trees (even ones in the middle of a field) are a benefit, as they provide shelter and shade for livestock. But from Charlie's standpoint, trees – like telegraph poles and pylons – represent a convenient and elevated perch for raptors and corvids to keep a daytime watch out for young and vulnerable partridges. There are already the woods and the hedgerows and, from Charlie's point of view at least, that will have to do, in terms of vegetation.

Water, for its own part, is a rare commodity on the chalky downs. There are no rivers, streams or natural ponds up here, so water needs to come either from rain, almost as it falls, or be stored in the series of dewponds that have been created around the farm. But the water that falls as rain out on the hills will inch its glacial way through the aquifers in the chalk, eventually making its way into the River Arun and the sea beyond after a number of years. Some of it will be intercepted once it reaches the surface, and will be abstracted from the stream to satisfy the needs of the local consumers and users. The less contaminated it is by added nitrates and other chemicals from farming, the better for the consumer, and the cheaper for the water company to process. For that reason, in an equation that will take well more than a decade to pay off, it is worth the company paying Conor to keep a hundred hectares or so out of production and leave them to an unimproved cover crop. That way, the cost of filtering the water is eventually reduced.

In a world of rapid decision-making and critical return on capital equations, it is somehow reassuring that it is going to take Southern Water around two decades to secure a payback on that policy, such is the holding capacity of the chalk aquifers.

The sun is dipping down towards the elevated horizon of Bury Hill, its orange glow shining on the faces of a small group standing between some cover crop and a wild-flower headland.

'So, you're not rewilding. You're not really intensive. So are you a regenerative farm, after all that?' asks someone of Conor, on one of the frequent farm visits that are set up on summer evenings. The question comes from a local farmer, who knows what he is asking and well understands the confusion that can come from relentlessly trying to apply terminology to things.

The question sets in train a lively discussion around the group as to what constitutes a regenerative farm and whether it really matters, anyway.

'I think so,' says Conor when the contributions eventually die down. 'Because we seem to follow all the principles. But I'm not sure that we do labels round here, so we've never really thought about it that way. All we're trying to do, at the end of the day, is leave the soil better than we found it.'

'And farm the hell out of the place for nature, of course,' adds Charlie.

11

DWELLERS ALL IN TIME AND SPACE: EARLY AUTUMN

Nothing here stays the same.

At dawn on a crisp September day Julie Ewald is staring out at the folds of land below her, slowly inking themselves into visibility. These stark chalkland downs are a far cry from the plains of the Nebraska mixed farm on which she was raised, and from which she first came to Britain on a Fulbright scholarship nearly three decades earlier. Her small team, many of them long retired from their day jobs, are waiting in their different start points for the light to be strong enough to begin the annual autumn stubble-count of grey partridges. It will be full-on for a couple of hours, and then they will all meet for breakfast and for companionship.

This is the fifty-fifth incarnation of those Sussex Study stubble-counts that Dick Potts instigated back in the 1960s, and which had led initially to his visit to Eddie all those years ago, and then to everything that had been done at Peppering ever since. Fifty-five years of information-gathering and sharing, of feeding results back to Natural England and out to all the other participating farmers. And year after year the study's findings have pointed to the same conclusion: namely, that widespread increased pesticide use leads to 'significant lower abundances of all groups of chick-food invertebrates'.[1] For the last twenty years the Sussex Study has been a useful tool with which the team at Peppering, which represents no more than 30 per cent of the total study area, can benchmark their own progress.

It's been Julie's project to lead for five years now, and she knows that the future value of the Sussex Study depends in large part on her moving it on, and not simply looking back at what her former boss would have done. So things have changed. The counting size has been cut down, for a start, mainly because it has become so difficult to see all the birds in all the wild-bird cover that criss-crosses the farm. Julie points out that, while Charlie's team (who do a separate count at the same time, to see what can responsibly be shot) has the luxury of thermal imagers, she doesn't; partly this is because the project is run on a shoestring and thermal imagers come in at about £3,000 each, and partly because continuity is everything for a long-term study, and having never had them in the past, they are not free to have them now. The land management has changed over large parts of the study area too. This is the result not so much of thick wads of scientific papers landing annually on farmers' doormats, but of the countless farmhouse-kitchen conversations that Julie herself conducts when the results are in, to make sure that the lessons are not lost and that they are subject to the correct interpretation. She knows, for example, that the indirect link between less insecticide use and more birdlife is best discussed over a cup of tea and not via a screen.

'That's the thing about a project like this,' she says. 'It rolls on for ever only so long as it stays useful. However thin the funding may be, however much there might be to do elsewhere in my working life, its value should increase with longevity, and not the other way around. The biggest decision now is who will take it on from me when I retire in ten years' time.'

Like Peppering, the boundaries of Julie's work are marked in time just as much as in space.

And, within that space, no land can be an island all of itself.

A sporting estate cannot live in isolation from its surrounding community, and, from the very start, Eddie wanted to make sure that the story of Peppering was told – told widely and told well.

This was an approach that immediately set them apart from most other shoots, and it had much to do with Eddie's belief that landowners are only ever life custodians of the land they own and that they have a duty of stewardship to hand it on in a better state at the end of their watch. It was also a logical long-term reaction to that 'Not on my watch' conversation that had taken place between Eddie and Dick Potts back in 2002 – an acknowledgement that the Peppering hill was a shared asset for the community. If the local community felt some sort of involvement in what was going on up the hill, it stood to reason that they would feel more invested in its success.

There were a number of reasons behind this, beyond the general need for the farm and the shoot to create and maintain cordial relations with the locals. This, after all, was where their beaters came from, and it was also a good recruiting ground for future employees of the estate. And, with good relations, word should filter back more immediately when things were going on that perhaps shouldn't be; beat keepers can roam far and wide at all hours of the day or night, but they can't be everywhere. 'Shooting is never going to please everyone,' was how Peter Knight's thinking went, 'but at least allow people to make up their own minds based on the facts, and in knowledge of the wider benefits to nature that our system of farming provides.' Furthermore, in this most de-natured corner of an already de-natured country, every person who could be inspired by what they saw and heard to take an interest, and even more so to change their own habits, or maybe get involved in a similar project themselves, was a huge bonus.

As soon as the team agreed that enough meaningful and visible progress had been made to make farm visits worthwhile, which was after about four years, they started inviting the locals in. In the winter this would take the form of indoor presentations, while in the summer it would be tractor and trailer rides around the farm, stopping at points of particular interest and always giving enough time for questions. One or more of the keepers would be available at stopping points to demonstrate specific points of interest, maybe to carry out an insect sweep and show the resulting contents on a white sheet, or to show the workings of one of the best-practice traps or restraints that were deployed around the place. Depending on the resources available at the time, there might be a total of four winter and four summer visits each year. The normal attendance at the start was around thirty to forty people (the latest one in 2022 was up to about seventy-five), so it was quite an exercise in logistics to get enough safe and comfortable transportation going, especially given that a fair percentage of attendees were not exactly in the first flush of youth. Once the visits were up and running, they were extended to special-interest groups, such as conservation, history and gardening clubs, each of which would have their own specific angles to examine.

Gradually the talks and visits morphed into something more specialist, and more to do with influencing and educating people, who could then go on to influence and educate others. Natural England, for example, has run training days at Peppering farm and has been an important part of them, as have been the relationships built up with campaigning organisations.

While this might have been an obvious step for the GWCT, from which Dick Potts came along all those years ago, visits from the RSPB, for instance, with its much more nuanced views on shooting, have been just as important. After one such of these in 2014, its then Director of Conservation, Mark Avery, wrote the following in his blog, under the heading 'Shooting – good for wildlife?': 'If we are talking native grey partridge rather than introduced red-legs or chukars then, when done at the top end of the game, as in Sussex on the Duke of Norfolk's land, it can be really, really good for a whole range of other farmland species. This isn't to say that all partridge shoots even approach that level, but fair's fair.'

For the team at Peppering, the tacit endorsement of a specialist, who has a very public profile on what he considers to be the 'wrong type of shooting', was both welcome and important. You don't have to approve of shooting to understand its potential contribution to the natural environment. The key lies in the word 'potential'.

A very important part of these talks and visits would be the question-and-answer sessions held at the end. In fact the team tend to regard these as the highlights, as they are a mark of how engaged people have felt, and they also give real-time feedback on the stuff that is going on. Sometimes these questions come from fellow farmers from the area, wanting to know the finer point of some conservation headland planting or a stewardship scheme; alternatively, there might be questions on bird densities or insect varieties, and changes in them since the beginning of the project. But one of the key topics always lies in the potentially awkward issue of predator control. The team knew, and accepted from the start, that plenty of people in the twenty-first century have genuine and heartfelt reasons to be uncomfortable with the notion of shooting and all that goes with it; thus it was not so much a question of trying to persuade them, so much as explaining why it was being done and reassuring them that it was being carried out to the highest possible welfare standards.

'Whatever else we did, we never ducked it,' said Peter. 'And we still don't now.'

It has not always been straightforward, by any means. On one occasion, when he went to address the Littlehampton Conservation Group at the District Council offices, Peter was met by two short lines of protesters dressed in badger costumes, passionately advocating for the rights of their animal to be recognised.

'I'm not sure that they realised we had never so much as laid a finger on a badger, nor would we ever. There was an uncomfortable silence, after which the badgers shuffled quietly off home.' But the wider point, which is that this is a world of many different and passionately held views, remains a strong one.

As the years have gone on, these events have developed more sophistication, in line with the public appetite for understanding exactly what is happening to the land around their homes. In 2022 an additional feature of one of the summer visits was to come and see for the first time the thirty-seven curlews from the headstarting project, still running around in their two large and secure runs and by now about two weeks from release.

It was an extraordinary moment to share, and the sense of occasion was not lost on the knowledgeable audience.

'I never thought I'd see the day,' said one elderly gentleman as he clambered back up the ladder and onto his straw-bale seat on the trailer. 'Curlews getting ready to fly over my own valley!'

In 2015 Peppering joined the Arun to Adur Farmer's Group, a voluntary cluster of thirty-eight farms of varying sizes that

Dwellers All in Time and Space: Early Autumn

covers nearly 11,000 hectares of the chalk downs between those two rivers, and which aims to deliver 'coordinated conservation benefits on a landscape scale'.[2]

This is important. As with any nature project that only operates within its own boundaries, there is a risk that it becomes a discrete island of biodiversity within a surrounding ocean of depletion. But biodiversity generally doesn't operate in isolation from its surroundings, and it will fail to thrive if it doesn't have other suitable local habitats to spread into, and effective corridors by which to get there. Many birds and mammals, in particular, have a natural disposition to travel surprising distances, and soon die out in, or move out of, an area that doesn't afford them the opportunity and means to do this.

The group was originally established, hosted and subsidised by Natural England within its Countryside Stewardship Scheme (CSS), but was then expected to make its own way voluntarily once it was fully up and running. That it succeeded in doing so, and in managing the transition based on the members paying an annual membership fee dependent on their size, speaks volumes, in Conor's reckoning, for the real commitment of local farmers to year-on-year improvement.

'Most people reckon we only ever do this sort of stuff when we are paid to by someone else, normally the taxpayer,' he says. 'Which isn't my own experience at all.'

It helped that the coordinator of the cluster first appointed by Natural England was none other than Colin Hedley who, in his other incarnation of specialist botanist, was a regular visitor to the farm and knew its biodiversity well, as well as that of the wider downland ecosystems. It fell to Colin to set in train the wide range of training events that would kick-start the knowledge base, and then the physical work, of changing things.

The idea was initially to make knowledge available that

enabled landowners and farmers to target specific aims, such as reducing their carbon footprint, improving the organic content of their soil, enhancing the quality of drinking water that filtered down through their land, and eventually end up with a better base from which to grow food profitably. By this means, they would also be increasing the long-term value and resilience of their own businesses and, quite literally, producing downstream benefits, such as improved drinking water and increased flood protection in the communities below them. They then selected a range of high-priority target species, such as the cornflower, the Duke of Burgundy butterfly, the water vole and the grey partridge, and set about creating the right environment within which each could thrive. Much of this eventual progress was enabled by a sharing-out of new resources, such as having access to the advice of expert agronomists whom they would not have been able to justify for their own needs and resources. These days the cluster organises training sessions and educational farm tours, and is currently working on a large-scale biodiversity mapping project across the whole area. The latest initiative is to get wild bird-feeders installed right across the group's area.

'In the future,' says Conor, 'we have the opportunity of going down the route of carbon sequestration and biodiversity net gain income from a far stronger standpoint collectively than if we were doing it on our own.'

An important part of what the Arun to Adur Farmer's Group sets out to do is to engage with the local communities and educate people on the importance of farming and farmland conservation. A 'Meet the farmer' project has been set up, along with little signs along the South Downs Way with QR codes that link to a video of local farmers explaining what they are doing, and what wildlife might be seen by people crossing their land.

This is all potentially time-consuming and expensive, and none of these schemes actually work in the long term if they can't demonstrate measurable progress. This one does. By 2019–20, for example, it was estimated that the combined effect of the group taking up the Southern Water land-management option on part of their land was an annual reduction of more than thirteen tonnes of nitrates into the ground water below. Recently, because of the amount of chalk grassland being specifically managed for the Duke of Burgundy butterfly, there has been a small increase in the population of an insect that has been declining in the area for decades.

Ultimately, much of the challenge is simply to get people communicating with each other again.

'I think restoring relationships with each other is critical to restoring our relationships with the land,' says Rick Goring, a neighbouring landowner and an early recipient of some of the surplus greys from Peppering. 'We don't all have the same views within the cluster, but it is an excellent forum for discussion, and sharing ideas and information of what has worked and, just as important, what hasn't.'

One of the ways in which Peppering has deliberately extended its outreach is through providing a place in which academic research is not only accepted, but also enthusiastically welcomed. The thinking goes that it is very likely that the team at Peppering can be helpful to the researcher, and even more likely that the researcher can provide useful specialist information back to the team, with everyone gaining in consequence. In many ways Peppering is a laboratory, and each little ecosystem is a Petri dish of potential and observable change. By virtue of the changes that have been made over the last twenty years, it offers a kind of scientific 'control' against which to ask the questions about how things might have been before the carnage of species loss got going.

For the last three years Ryan Burrell, a specialist field worker and researcher into the declines of wading birds, has been conducting work on Peppering towards his PhD on the potential impact of the recovering raptor populations. It is one of three sites for the project, and has been chosen specifically because of the recent vibrant recovery of raptors up to a level where they are capable of making a meaningful dent in the numbers of prey species. Rather like Dick Potts before him, Ryan has become part of the furniture on the study site that is known as 'Peppering C', frequently spending hours making notes, assessing evidence and setting webcams. He is a fine field worker, and Charlie's view is that you can't have too many good field workers around the place, especially if they drop in for a coffee and tell you what they have been noticing.

'Generally,' says Ryan, 'what is good for the breeding partridge is good for the breeding lapwing, so we would expect to find decent overall conditions.' The exception, he points out, is that partridges are birds of the hedges and margins, whereas the lapwing prefers the open spaces in the middle of spring tillage and fallow ground. In a way the lapwing would probably prefer the country to be a bit more open and the farming to be much more traditional and mixed. This latter point helps to explain why the lapwing has had such a pitiful few decades nationally, during which it has had to compete not only with chemicals and disturbance, but also with winter wheat blocking out the lines of sight through which it would normally get early warning of ground predators. After all, the entire nest survival strategy of a lapwing is based on a clear enough view to enable sufficient early warning, with the sitting parent having a long enough time to rise up in the air and begin its act of diversion before a predator finds the nest and eats the chicks.

Ryan's birds nest slightly earlier than the partridges and fledge by mid-June. Whereas for the partridge it is the weather during Ascot week that determines much of the success of the season, with lapwings it tends to be a month earlier, around the early-May bank holiday. He shares evidence from the nest cameras with Charlie, pointing out that the principal recent predators have been crows and foxes. 'One tiny thing that we have found about foxes', he says, as a random observation, 'is that they can detect infrared light much better than us, often staring hard at the camera as if trying to understand where the light is coming from.'

Ryan is not the only academic on the farm. Julie comes up to do her Sussex Study counts in early September; someone else has done a master's degree on the corn bunting; and a second PhD candidate has been looking at lapwing camouflage, involving micro-habitat selection (meaning exactly at what height the nest is sited), and whether birds have the innate ability to match eggs to the precise habitat.

When all is said and done, Ryan's study birds at Peppering have proved to be an island of success in a sea of surrounding decline. Over the three-year period that he has been coming, the number of chicks successfully fledged has risen to an average of 1.3 per nest. This productivity rate, if reproduced nationally, would swiftly lift the bird off the Red List as a UK bird of conservation concern.

But then it is not for nothing that at least a dozen birds on that same list – from linnets to yellowhammers, and from swifts to corn buntings – can be seen in abundance at the appropriate time of year all over the farm. Around 45 per cent of all worldwide biodiversity decline is down to straightforward habitat loss,[3] and up to about 80 per cent of that to farming itself, so it is not surprising what happens if farming is once again carried out with nature in mind.

That's why Ryan chose Peppering. It is also why everyone around here harbours a hope that one day soon a PhD student will be able to study the turtle dove here.

Nothing here stays the same, not even in the basic architecture of the land.

Fifteen miles of hedges remained the vital arterial highways of the farm's biodiversity and, in the early autumn, the team agreed on an entirely new protocol for their management. It had arisen as a follow-on from the joint meeting of the ecologists back in the spring.

In terms of cutting, this was reduced down to one side each year, so that the two-year-old wood on the uncut side would continue to provide food for the berry-eaters, like redwings and fieldfares, during the harder months of autumn and winter. Where hedges were becoming bare underneath, they would be laid; this entailed cutting part of the way through leading shoots at about five centimetres from the ground and then laying them over, staking them in, so as to encourage new vertical growth from the boughs and new horizontal growth from the trunk. This, in turn, provided vital impenetrable cover in the future for songbirds such as warblers, nightingales, dunnocks and whitethroats, particularly when they were at their most vulnerable in the winter.

Graeme (the entomologist) had recommended new six-metre grass margins on the south side of hedges, complete with wild flowers, designed to provide a warmer microclimate for insects. If you were to take a cross-section of, say, just one metre of the resulting hedge with its new margin, you would find a

Dwellers All in Time and Space: Early Autumn

total of no fewer than ten species of hedging plant,[4] four of grass in the beetle bank down below[5] and thirty-one types of flower and grass in the new margins[6] – and all of that before the arrival of any of the usual arable weeds that would blow in over the coming months. Forty-five different types of plant deliberately set in the immediate area of one metre of hedging. And each of these forty-five plants has a slightly different range of insects and birds that it attracts, leading to a deeper and wider overall contribution to the bounty of the place. It was an expensive and time-consuming exercise (around £3,000 per hectare, for which admittedly grants were available), but it demonstrated the lengths that are gone to in order to ensure that Peppering has the widest possible biodiversity and bio-abundance.

Nothing sits still here. It can't, because nature doesn't.

This could all be extremely challenging in its complexity, with all those communities of organisms coming together to create local populations that operate alongside each other in one ecosystem that borders many others. Or, when you remember that nature has been doing all this without human help since the dawn of time, it can be almost childishly simple. By managing human activity in a way that mimics nature, rather than competes with or ignores it, it turns out that life floods quickly back.

'You don't need a PhD in Life Sciences', says Eddie, as he stares down one of the new grass margins at the north end of the farm, 'to understand that things will get better if we take our feet off nature's throat. In a way, that's all we've done here. We've had to manage the process. It's been expensive, it's been time-consuming and sometimes it has been very frustrating. But twenty years later, the whole place is alive again. Just think what it could be like in another twenty years. What we have done here at Peppering is not rocket science, but it is attention to detail in a massive, concentrated way, and it takes a huge amount of human effort to make all of this happen. It takes persistence, courage and humility, because nature is greater than all of us.'

12

LEE FARM: MID-AUTUMN

Planning is bringing the future into the present so that you can do something about it now.

Alan Lakein

Estates, like empires, rise and fall over the decades and centuries. They are inveterate shapeshifters.

Land is bought, land is sold; fields make way for villages and roads; families go in different directions and take parcels of land with them. Dynasties gain and lose fortunes. In short, things happen.

Ever since he inherited the Norfolk title, Eddie had been keen to bring the disparate parts of the old estate together again, part of a vision that he hoped could eventually create one of the great traditional partridge manors in the country. In 2020 an opportunity to take almost 700 hectares back in hand arose across the eastern boundary. In fact the opportunity was for more than double that, but the part that made sense from the farming, shooting and conservation point of view was Lee Farm. The remainder, to the south, was quite heavily wooded and therefore not suitable, but Lee Farm was a logical extension to Peppering in every way.

The deal involved buying out the last seven years of the sitting-contract farmer, a relatively expensive transaction, but one that needed to be concluded quite quickly, given the time it would then take to plan the new farming, build new beetle banks, plant twenty miles of hedging with a view to attracting the greys down the hill from Peppering. Anything that had previously been reared there would either go feral or die off, before the first shot was fired under the new regime. From the start, there was no question of bringing any birds in from elsewhere, but rather of creating the environment and conditions into which they would come of their own volition, as they had already been doing – albeit patchily – over the last decade. 'Ten becomes twenty,' explained Charlie, 'which becomes forty, which becomes eighty, which becomes two hundred, and suddenly you've got the makings of a shootable surplus.'

Only when the deal looked certain to go ahead, in the early summer of 2022, did Eddie dare to ask Charlie and Conor to come and sit with him up on the hill and start the planning process of where the new field divisions would go and where the drives would be, which would dictate where the hedges and beetle banks would be sited. This was an exercise in new land management on a grand scale, both an opportunity and a challenge. On the way back to Peppering, Charlie told the Duke that this new patch would need the employment of not one but two new beat keepers; the team of three at Peppering were already stretched as it was, particularly as one of the existing beats was already covered by Charlie, who clearly didn't have the time to take on any extra work at all.

Thus, by late summer Jack and Niall had been joined by Arron and Dom, while in the office Conor and Sue were getting to grips with a cropping plan.

Suddenly, Peppering was 40 per cent bigger than before.

Being bigger meant many things, but more than anything, it

Lee Farm: Mid-Autumn

meant that the land could be managed and farmed on more of a landscape scale, and that the conditions that had worked so well for wildlife across Peppering for the last twenty years would now have the benefit of twice the area in which to replicate themselves. The general rule in nature is that the bigger the 'island', the more varied the biodiversity; by the same token, as the great biologist Edward O. Wilson[1] pointed out decades ago, the smaller the island, the more fragile its ecosystem.

With the hectares of new land that had been brought into his farm, and all the work this would entail, Conor was surprisingly relaxed about it all. Having been brought up on a nearby small family farm, and then having cut his commercial teeth running a large and prominent organic farm on the other side of the Downs, change was something that excited rather than daunted him. Change, done right, meant opportunity.

'It's a bit rough up at the top,' he said, referring to the flint fields that Nick would be shortly asked to go and create beetle banks on, 'but the main ground is good. It's lower than ours, for a start, and it's had a huge amount of organic matter put on it over the last decade or so. Apart from that, the access is better and, even if the average field size is bigger than we want at the moment, they are well laid out and give us plenty of potential to work with.' In terms of buildings, he had a sheep shed, a barn, a grain drier and a few storage facilities. In a way, money had been less tight at Lee Farm than at Peppering, as the business of farming had not been qualified and driven by what was good for the partridges. Lee Farm had simply been about being a profitable farm. The trick now would be to keep the profitability, wherever possible, while delivering on stewardship that would, in turn, deliver on biodiversity.

'Besides,' said Conor, 'it's amazing how many of the Peppering birds have leaked down here over the years, particularly when things have got a bit crowded up on the hill. It's not as if we're needing to try to do anything against the grain.'

The immediate change would, of course, be on the edges of the fields, where the existing Higher Level Stewardship schemes would be replaced by Countryside Stewardship schemes, which would take around eighteen metres out of each field's perimeter – taking into account where three bands met, including grass strip, wild-bird seed mix and unsprayed conservation headland. Then the block cropping plan would change to a patchwork one, with a shorter rotation than the one up at Peppering (there being no rotational grass leys), moving from winter wheat to spring barley to winter beans or some other cover crop. Conor's plan was also to bring more science into improving the soil, with a soil-testing regime that started with every hectare being tested, by way of providing a baseline that would last for the next four years, and then randomised testing in between to provide the scientific base for further improvement.

Regarding livestock, there was already a resident flock of sheep at Lee Farm, and the decision was taken to allow the owner to keep grazing them, rather than increase the size and complexity of Martin's operation back at Peppering. Finally Conor would call in the 'flint harvesters' from time to time – people who would remove a tonnage of flint from the higher fields for free and then profit from using it in house-building. Last time he had brought them in, they had recovered 1,100 tonnes of flint from just twenty hectares of the farm. This not only made the fields easier to work, but also saved a fortune in replacing drillheads.

The nature of modern farming reflects a relentless 100-year process of replacing manpower with machinery, for good or ill. Back in 1914 around 5 per cent of Britain's workforce was employed on farms, a figure that is now a shade over 1 per cent;

Lee Farm: Mid-Autumn

and it was a sign of the way things were that neither Conor, as the farm manager, nor Nick, as the main contractor, found it necessary to employ any extra people to cover the extra hectares at Lee Farm. Nick could upgrade to bigger and more capable machinery, while Conor could bring in expertise (like the soil-testing) as and when he needed it, but could stick with the lean payroll for the everyday jobs.

A charm of about forty goldfinches burst south out of the hedgerow as Nick Field came into the seventeen-hectare block of land known as 'Dog Leg', followed by the dark sickle-shape of the hobby that was chasing them. It was a kind of instant reward for the long trek up from his yard to the most distant corner of the expanded estate. The hedges that he had passed on his way up were already heavy with rosehips, blackberries and sloes, little colourful signallers of the changing seasons and shortening days.

Dog Leg was part of the area of Lee Farm that he would now be contract-farming, in preparation for which he had steadily upgraded and upsized his machinery over the winter and spring so that he could cope with the extra work more or less on his own. It was land that was already familiar to him, as he had gazed across to it from Peppering over the last two decades, and across its borders he had often cooperated with the previous contractor. Fundamentally it was the same hard chalk downland that he was used to, only its fields were still enormous, and the top of the farm reached right up to the fringes of the South Downs Way, the iconic footpath that runs for 100 miles along the ridge between Eastbourne in the east and Winchester in the west. From his own little dairy herd down at Splash Farm, he had come a long way in the last twenty years, at once alongside and utterly intertwined with the Peppering Project. It never failed to amaze him that, these days, he did much of his farming from the cab of a highly computerised £150,000 beast of a tractor.

The last time he had included the preparation of beetle banks in his daily work, twenty years earlier, he had been towing a little plough behind a much smaller tractor; now he had a vast ten-tonne, 285-horsepower tractor to do the job. Back then, Peter Knight had walked behind him, sowing the grass over the beetle bank with a traditional fiddle; this time it would be as automated as possible, in preparation for no fewer than twenty miles of hedging that were scheduled to go in over the winter.

As Nick watched the hobby flying off empty-handed down into the valley below, he considered how much all this had changed since those early days, and how it was something that was in many ways supplementary to food production, but still critical to the increase of biodiversity. Ploughing the soil slightly uphill into the form of a bank, hard by the South Downs Way, wasn't exactly straightforward. For one thing, it was a time-consuming job during one of the busiest times of the farming year, a process of slow passes and re-passes down the 500-metre boundary of the field, as the soil gradually worked its way into shape. Second, it was just about the hardest ground in the area, full of flints of ever-increasing size that jolted and jarred the ploughshare as it went down deeper with each pass. Those flints would eventually have the last word on the state of the expensive metal shares, which would often need replacing as he progressed, and on the massive tyres that would be grooved and ridged by the constant abrasion of the sharp stones. Finally, it was thirsty work for the tractor, which would easily get through 500 litres of diesel in a long day of building the banks, in a world where the cost of any sort of fuel had rocketed in the last year.

Lee Farm: Mid-Autumn

Each pass went deeper until, on the fifth, he could look back on a serviceable bank and move on to the next one. Nick would be back here in only a couple of weeks to drill the winter barley, and he knew the Duke would inspect every bit of his work to ensure the bank was high enough for partridges to nest on, and that the length of the hedge was exactly right.

This time in, say, five years, he thought to himself as he headed down the hill to the next proposed beetle bank, there would be 500 metres of mixed hedging running along the downhill side of the South Downs Way. On the one hand, there would be the loss, for 500 metres, of an inspiring view across the coastal plain and out to the English Channel for walkers and cyclists; on the other, their journeys would be enriched by the extraordinary uplift in biodiversity and bio-abundance that would surely follow.

The work at Lee Farm would have many consequences, but one would be the doubling or trebling of the number of passers-by on the National Trail who would have the opportunity to share in the new bounty. Sharing in it meant talking about it. And talking about it meant spreading the renaturing word ever wider, which was one of the original aims.

But it is now the time of year to go back to the beginning of the story and remind ourselves that it all started off for the benefit of just that one bird.

13

SHOOT DAY: AUTUMN

For a man whose entire year's work could be said to be judged on the basis of the results of one day, it might seem strange that head keeper Charlie Mellor's recurring nightmare, ahead of his annual grey partridge shoot day, is nothing more than that he might oversleep.

'I dream', he says, 'that I have woken up at about ten o' clock with sixty missed calls on my phone, and a sharp banging on the door.'

The reality is that he is always up and about at least two hours before he needs to be. Generally he is able to organise two days out with the greys for the Duke and his guests each season, and on occasions as many as three, but in a year when the rains have fallen incessantly throughout June, as they have this year, the all-important shootable surplus is only ever going to allow for one day, and even that will be a short one. There are some self-imposed rules in this kind of project that never get bent or broken and, in the face of plenty of temptation, this is one of them. Shooting may have driven the project, but it is always still subservient to nature.

In mid-September, when the harvest was in, Charlie, the Duke and the beat keepers had done their painstakingly careful stubble-counts, field by half-lit field, dawn by silent dawn. Morning after morning they were out there staring through night-vision scopes, with a hierarchy of hopes that began, maybe, with the frequent sighting of pairs with multiple young, and ended with a few barren pairs flitting across the furrows in front of them. Once done, Charlie put the recording of what amounted to every single covey on the estate onto a spreadsheet and divided the total number of young by the total number of hens which would give him the first firm indication of what the surplus would be. It had been a tough season; not disastrous by any means, but tough. Of the red grouse's six eggs, as many as five will normally survive to fledge, whereas with the grey partridge, fourteen eggs will routinely reduce to just three adults. At the other end of the scale, ocean-going seabirds have a one-egg strategy that concentrates all the family resources over a quarter of the year into the new life on a rock ledge or down a burrow; generally, at least in the absence of foxes and rats, it works for them. Nature is like that: evolution has led species towards very different breeding strategies, but it is often man who enables them to work or not.

The British weather is a good place to start the process of understanding. The rain that poured down during Ascot week kept on falling from the skies throughout the month of June, in a way that reduced the productivity of each breeding pair, almost by the hour. So Charlie can offer one day of shooting. Just one day in which the fruits of the skills and dedication of himself and his team will be there for all to see. One day when the efforts of the whole estate – the beat keepers, the farm workers, the fence-menders and vermin-trappers, the hedge-layers and harvesters, the tractor drivers and scientists – will either prove to have worked or not. One day that can be spoiled or ruined by heavy rain, thick fog, high wind, an impatient dog, a hungry fox or even the delaying effects of heavy traffic. One day to enjoy all that they have worked so hard to achieve, and to appreciate the biodiversity far beyond the game birds hurtling over the high hedges. One day that sticks a metaphorical flag in the soil and announces, 'This is who we are, what we do and this is what we have achieved together.'

In the wide sweep of the estate's combined efforts, there are countless other things that make up the year – the Castle, the farm, the cottages, the park, the cricket, the ongoing projects and the community relations, for example – but it is the wild shoot that has been the driver of all that has been done to allow the biodiversity to thrive alongside it. Since those first days of field sports, when some Elizabethan man in a punt initially discharged his breech-loading gun into a flock of ducks a metre or so above the water, the pursuit of shooting a flying bird has amounted to far more than the sum of its parts. It often grew to be the principal function of a country estate; more recently it has become the entire commercial axle around which some of these estates have rotated – captives, as they then often become, to the requirement to bring in ever more reared birds than the land can sensibly hold, so as to cover the ever-increasing costs involved. If steps aren't taken to avoid it, a day can become a numbers game, the rural playing out of a high-value transaction between money and land, with nature a mere incidental backdrop, and often a declining one at that.

But here, it is not about numbers. Shooting is the owner's dividend from an ecosystem of a patch of land that has been invested in, trodden lightly upon and allowed to thrive to the beat of its natural rhythms. In principle, Charlie has about two months from when the exact date is selected to get all the details in place. Then, once he knows roughly from where the wind is likely to blow, he agrees with the Duke, in precise detail, the eight drives and the order in which they will be done, being roughly from upwind to downwind. Wild partridges are notoriously more difficult to manage than, say, reared pheasants,

Shoot Day: Autumn

and the aim of presenting them equally over a line of eight guns that is maybe only 250 metres from one end to another requires decades of understanding of where, and how, they will tend to want to fly and, equally important, where they won't. It starts with the siting of the pegs for the individual guns, a combination of tradition, weather forecasting and hunch; the keeper's skill is to aim to fly the birds over the most windward of the eight guns, in the knowledge that they will then slide down the wind to offer a decent shot for more than one gun. With eight drives, this means that sixty-four pegs need to be positioned to the nearest metre, and then shifted if and when the weather – or the boss – dictates.

Grey partridges are alert to danger all the time, and the accidental early spotting of just one gun by one partridge behind the high hedgerows can send the whole covey careening back through a gap in the line of flankers. The old ones are the smartest, the ones who have seen all this before in an earlier season, for which the smarting collective memory of 'broken toes and family bereavements' serves as an urgent incentive to avoid danger, and to keep others away from it as well. They are the shapeshifters, the gap-finders and the spotters of weakness. It is for this reason that Charlie needs a small army of beaters and flankers who know what they are doing.

Such is the attraction and rarity of a traditional day on grey partridges that he has no problem at all in recruiting the fifty or so experienced beaters that he needs. Indeed, more than half of those will be other gamekeepers who have taken days off from their own shoots to participate, so much so that 1 per cent of all the gamekeepers in Britain will be on that one 800-hectare patch of land on the day in question. And it is a passionate coming-together. From all corners of the country they come – from the grouse moors of North Yorkshire to the beech hangers of Hampshire, from the Weald of Kent to the wilds of Wiltshire – all in their own uniform of estate tweeds. Those who mistake the scene as a feudal one in which a large number of people serve up entertainment for a small and privileged gun line often fail to understand that, for just about everyone, simply being there, and being part of a giant exercise of working with the grain of nature, transcends the routine normality of a working life. For some people, who themselves work with wild partridges, it presents the chance to see how it should be done on a significant scale, and against the beautiful backdrop of the South Downs and the River Arun flowing into the sea. For many of them, though, this will be a rare opportunity to see the kind of wild-bird day that their grandfather might have seen, and it is more holiday than work.

Not for Charlie and his beat keepers, it isn't. The previous fortnight is a whirl of mowing strips and cutting holes in hedges for the beater to pass through, of flailing brushwood and valeting Land Rovers, of topping and scything, of filling water butts and strimming around feeders, of positioning and then repositioning pegs and always, always, of constantly looking at the most trusted of their long-range weather apps. A few days before, Charlie is out with his four beat keepers, the ones who will supervise each of the beating teams, settling on the precise sequencing of who will be where when, where the flankers will stand, and who needs to be somewhere else before the first one can move on again. By the end of the session, you could draw a map if you wanted to, with the precise lines of advance and the timings of each beater, each flanker and each dog; but a beat keeper's knowledge of his own patch is intimate, encyclopaedic even, and there is no need for a map. Charlie looks up momentarily and sees a goshawk fly high over one of the stubble fields, as much a welcome sign of the remorseless returning of nature

Shoot Day: Autumn

onto the farm as it is a relentless killer of game birds, both on the ground and in the air. Twenty years ago there were no goshawks. But then there were virtually no grey partridges either. Here, both are a welcome part of the circle of life and death.

As he returns home in the last rays of the autumn sun, Charlie has a number in his mind, but he is not telling anyone. This is not about numbers, though, so much as it is about a feeling that the year's work has worked out and borne fruit.

Dawn, and silence.

But it is a silence within which a thousand interconnected things are happening. Out there in the fields and hedges and skies around and above, and in this season of mists and mellow fruitfulness, the silence is always stirring to be heard.

Two early-morning red kites quarter the Church Field for any casualties that the night may have brought. In the valley a skein of early Canada geese rise up from the damp meadows to seek their daytime living on the stubbles above. Strands of traveller's joy lie across the hedgerow by Peppering Farm lane, waving imperceptibly in the breath of the wind. No part of this nature is too small to delight, and none is too insignificant not to be part of a vast, unseen connectivity.

Charlie, predictably, has been up since long before dawn. For 360 or so days of the year he is perhaps more resident estate ecologist than he is head gamekeeper, but on the remaining handful, he very much has to revert to his original job description. Even in this young modern world, and with a young modern keeper, there is no substitute for the scientific precision and military control that go with a day of driven wild grey partridge shooting.

In theory (but only in theory) his plan is straightforward. On his laminated map he has eight lines of about 250 metres each, over which – in the eight different phases of the day, the drives – all he has to do is push birds that are evenly spaced both in distribution and time. He starts with an intimate knowledge of how the grey partridge thinks, how it will probably behave on the ground and in the air, and where it is likely to fly, relative to the wind direction. He knows how it will spot gaps, react to flags and slide down contours; that it will sit tight to the ground among the wet turnips and out in the stubble until the last moment. He knows how it immediately sees the weakness of a corner in a line, and that he must therefore create lines that bend with soft curves. For the fourteen years he has been here, Charlie has watched these birds day by day and has learned about their habits; he has seen how the old cock birds will instinctively try to lead the covey away from trouble. As the hedges have grown, he has seen how the flight lines have changed imperceptibly. He knows how far the greys will fly, how often in a day and how long he has, once a covey has been moved to a new area before it will start to make its own way back home. Above all, he knows that the grey will fly more elusively, and less predictably, than a red-legged partridge – as much a challenge for the keeper as it is for the guns.

As he crosses the yard to the kennels in the half-light, Charlie notices two late-summer swallows above the telegraph lines, the continent of Africa still weeks away in their distant evolutionary map, and they remind him that it will be unseasonably hot in a few hours' time.

He is lucky, in two senses. First, in the management of expectations, in that his employer and his guests are, at heart, country people and they well understand that things can, and do, stray from the plan with wild birds in uncertain autumnal weather conditions. Second, the many people who help him try to achieve as good a day as they can are mainly experts themselves, well versed in what needs to be done and what is expected of them. They are professionals who want it to succeed as much as he does, from the old retired keepers who walk stiffly into their positions as flankers, to Charlie's twelve-year-old godson, who has been coming here all his life, but for whom this is the first time he has been allowed on 'the big one'. It will be a minor truancy stuffed full of education.

Two hours before the shoot is due to begin, the beaters start arriving, out from where the morning mists wreathe ribbons across the River Arun in the low, slanting sunlight. They come in their Land Rovers, their Land Cruisers and their battered old station wagons; they come with their spaniels, loaded with the kinetic energy of raw, suppressed excitement; they come with their overnight stubble and flat caps, their banter and their stories. All around them the yard fills with the tools of the day: the tractors, seconded from farm work for the day to tow beaters' trailers; the purple boxes with drinking water and flags – white, orange or red, depending on what their user's function is; the tea urn and the paper cups; the box of radios and the list of the drives to come. A buzzard slides overhead in the faint breeze.

Once he has briefed them on safety and the coming day, Charlie reads out who will be in which group of beaters and flankers, for all the world like names in a school roll call. It is a chance for his two young beat keepers, Niall and Jack, to practise their leadership on groups of beaters who are often old enough to be their fathers, people who started all this on the far side of yesterday, but who will listen intently and play the game. No one wants this to fail.

'Let's see what we have at lunch,' says Charlie, when a beater asks what bag he is after. He has a few small contingency plans up his sleeve, but this is down to nature.

The Return of the Grey Partridge

Meanwhile, at breakfast in the main house, the talk is of the wildness that sets this day apart, that makes it so special an invitation. Years ago, and often since, Eddie had articulated to the team his ambition that he would one day be able to say to his guests at the shoot-day breakfast that everything that would come over the guns would be wild, and absolutely nothing reared. Now he has achieved that. He understood the privilege he had, to have made this happen, as much as he understood the obligation he felt to allow nature back in, to enable it. Just as for Charlie, for whom it was the culmination of a year of hard work and planning, so for Eddie it was the realisation of a twenty-year dream. As he took his gun from the cabinet, he momentarily found himself thinking of Dick Potts and wishing that he was still around to see it.[1] Dick was not a shooting man himself, but the sight of those coveys of greys hurtling in numbers over the new hedgerows, where once there had been neither hedge nor partridge, would have delighted him.

Then there is a bursting into life of a score of engines, and the convoy moves off to its various drop-off points for the first drive. If there is a tension, it is one that is muted with the confidence that comes from experience. If there is nervousness, it is only because nature in the raw will do what she will do, whether it suits us or not. Up on the hedged hillside there are a hundred hectares of ground, an area maybe the size of 250 football pitches, to bring in from both sides and from behind; the whole skyline has pinprick figures moving towards each other. Most of them have large white plastic flags on wooden poles, which they flap noisily at ground level from time to time through the damp headlands. The flankers have orange and red flags. Down in the valley below, the eight guns walk quietly towards their pegs; they are fine shots, but then they will need to be.

Shoot Day: Autumn

As the lines close in on each other, Charlie's voice crackles through the various radios with a stream of fine adjustments, little delays and exhortations to keep in contact with the people on the flanks. Soon they are close enough to hear him without radios.

'Keep in line!' he shouts at the left-hand group of beaters – no radio required.

'Oh, he's off,' chuckles one of the older keepers, holding back, as he has been asked. 'I'm amazed that he has kept quiet for so long.'

A hare that has been disturbed in its furrow on the right-hand side runs in a lazy arc uphill and towards the back of the line, before choosing a gap to run through and accelerating slightly to pass through it. In a mirror image, another hare, darker this time, does the same thing from the left. Later on, one of the retired keepers says that he has never seen so many hares in one place in his life.

The first grey partridge of the day, a lone surviving cock from the previous season, flies low towards the beaters and away from the gun line.

'Flags!' shouts Charlie. 'Get those bloody flags up!' Sometimes, he says, you just have to charge at the partridges to turn them. He adds, to no one in particular, that he needs a little more breeze for things to be perfect. Too much wind is chaos, too little is like herding cats; force two to three on the Beaufort scale is ideal.

Later in the day, and probably with younger birds, the beaters and their flags will become more and more effective at turning the greys back towards the guns, but not now. The old cock bird is not to know that there will only be one day's shooting on the manor this year, but he will still be about at the end of it and possibly for the start of another season, in another year. He passes serenely back over the right-hand group of beaters and towards the safety of the stubble, two fields to the north. No beater or flanker grudges him a longer life.

Everything then waits a minute for a walker on a footpath. She will never know that, behind a dozen hedgerows, a small army of hidden beaters is standing quietly still, to let her walk out of the way at her own pace.

A few pheasants fly high over the gun line unchallenged. It is not about them today, and the guns have been asked to let them through. On the extremes of the two groups nearest the guns, the experienced flankers signal the approach of the partridges with shrill whistles, one for a single bird, two for a couple and a continual blast for a large covey. Later on at lunch, one of the guns swears blind that the whistling is louder and more excited if the approaching bird is a grey, rather than a red-legged partridge. 'It *is* louder,' says one of the old flankers, laying his red flag down in the back of the trailer, 'because that's what I bloody want it to be.'

When the first large covey flies over the hedge, and the initial shots are fired, the covey star-bursts into the sky upwards and outwards like the military jets at an air show. It is for this instant of star-burst, for this primeval expression of utter wildness, that they have all been working for the last year. If any one display of the raw and natural will to survive sums up the last two decades of work in this place, it is that heavenward burst of energy. This is almost as far as it is possible to get from the lumbering straight flight of a reared pheasant out of some maize, plunging down into the hedges beyond. Then the separated covey passes on across the steep hill beyond, unbroken. Even the best shots need to get their bearings.

And these are some of the best in Britain. They have to be, because the greys are phenomenally hard targets. Because there

Shoot Day: Autumn

is a respect for the quarry here, a respect that says that birds should either be left or killed, but not wounded; a respect that insists that every shot bird is picked up, taken to someone's home and eaten. A grey partridge hurtling over a three-metre hawthorn hedge above a grassy valley is as unlike a clay pigeon as wine is unlike beer.

Ten minutes later the drive is over. Where the beaters generally have spaniels, the pickers-up have Labradors; they have been hidden from sight until Charlie's horn signifies the end of the drive, and now they are released. The easier of the fallen partridges that have landed on the grass are picked by the guns themselves; it is in the chaotic tangle of blackthorn bushes in front of the pegs, and in the scrub behind them, that those dogs will earn their corn. Some of them will still be there long after the next drive has started behind some other hedge, and in some other valley.

The day wears on. After the breathless and bright calm of the early morning, the northwesterly breeze picks up, and the sun becomes hazy behind a screen of thin cloud. Kestrels move from hedge to hedge, seemingly unaware of the loudness of the action around them, heads down and alert only to the tiny infrared trails that will lead them to their prey down below. Red kites slide down the wind, and huge charms of goldfinches explode from one thicket to the next. Different widths of trail through the headlands indicate where rats, badgers or hares have commuted in and out over the weeks and months for their daily foraging. There are around ninety people involved today, transient visitors into a world of plenty that about half a dozen of them have created.

Much later, the arrival of the beating line at the far side of the hedge where the guns are standing signifies that the last drive is nearly done and the day is shortly going to come to an end. Flags beat a little more lethargically now, and the chatter is a bit louder, in the knowledge that this day that is ending has been a good one – a great one even. There is contentment on both sides of that hedge when suddenly a partridge, an old cock, bursts up from underneath the very feet of a beater in the wild-flower mix and flies high over the gun line towards a neighbouring copse. No one fires a shot, and the horn duly blows.

'One for next year,' says Eddie, breaking his gun and removing the cartridges. It is a season that has lasted one day, but he is sublimely content.

High above, a pair of marsh harriers drift down the late-afternoon breeze, solid and strong in the October sunshine. A green woodpecker yaffles its way down the same arc as the last partridge flew, just minutes before.

And slowly, one by one, vehicle by vehicle, the guns, the beaters, the flankers, the loaders, the drivers and the pickers-up leave the stage. Almost the last to go is an eighty-five-year-old cherry farmer from Kent. Every year, come rain or shine, he drives sixty miles for this day, to walk slowly around after each drive with his magnetic stick collecting the spent cartridges, and then sixty miles back again. He will go on doing it until he can no longer walk.

'While the legs hold out,' he says, when he is asked if he will be back again next year. 'And if I'm spared.'

From high above on the escarpment you can just about see the exhausted dogs lying flat on the grass, and can smell the smoke from a handful of cigarettes and hear the laughter gently ebbing and flowing like a sea tide.

Charlie convenes his small team of beat keepers and breaks into an uncomplicated smile.

'Good work,' he says. 'I think we did okay.'

PART THREE
Tomorrow

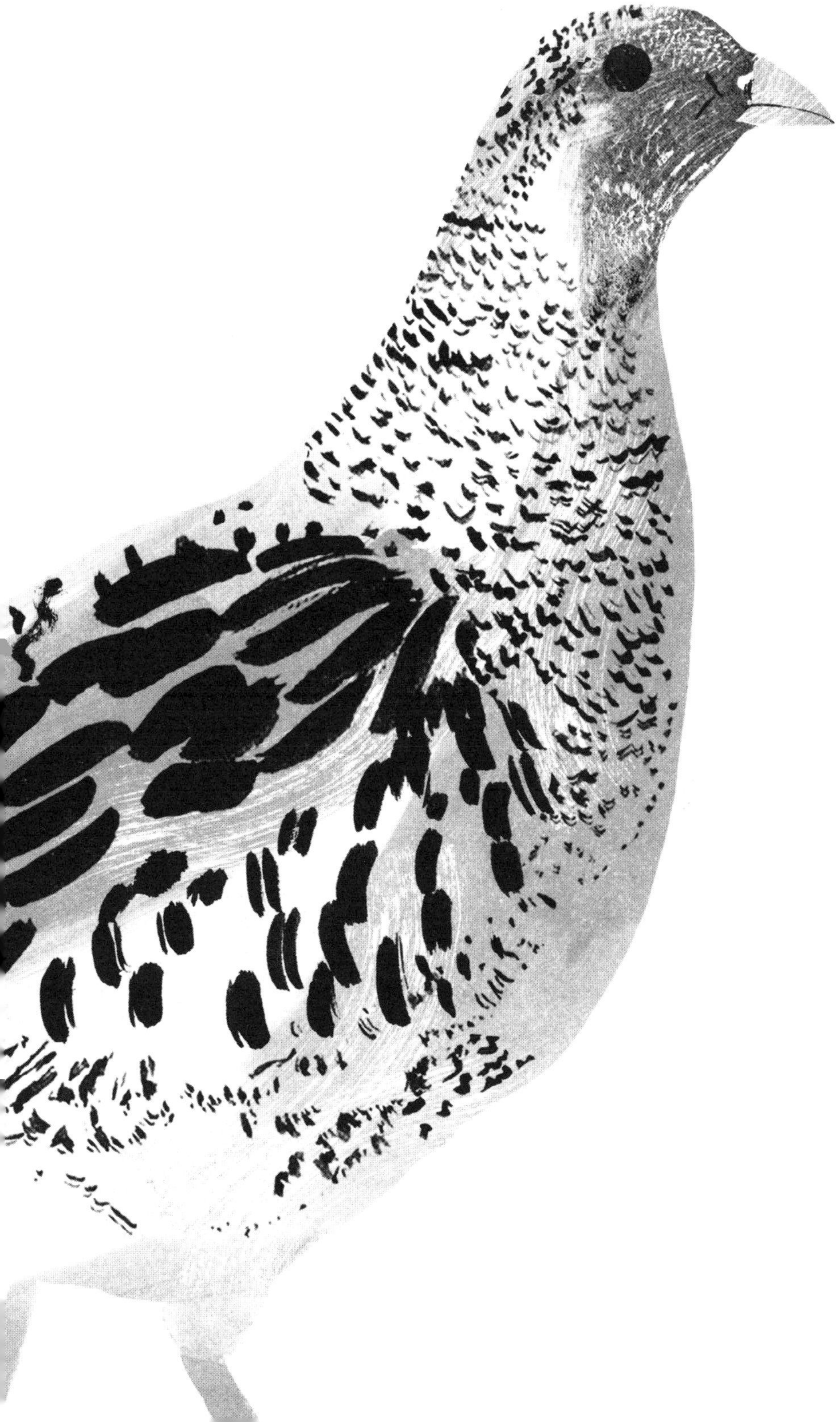

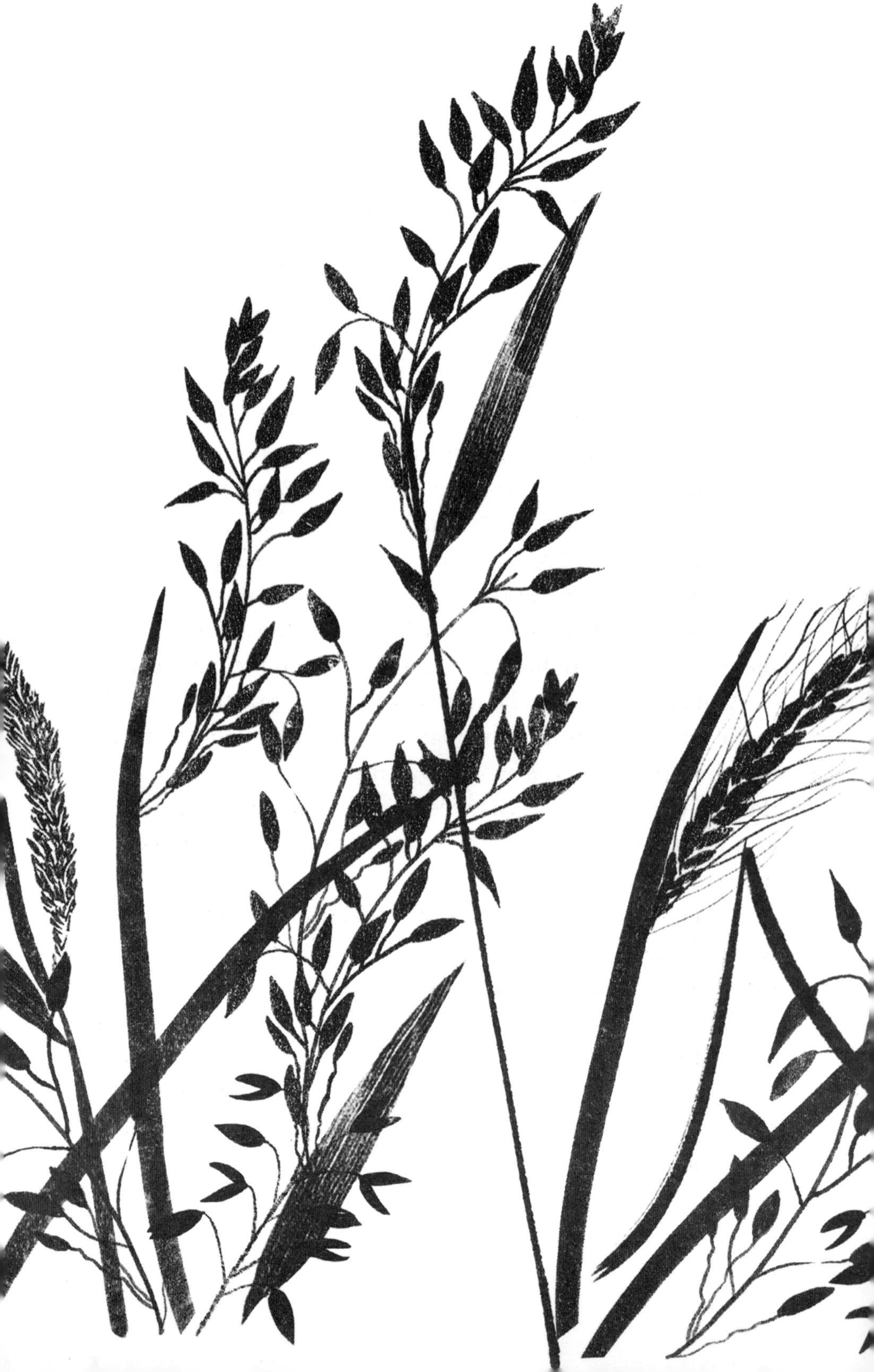

14

WHERE NEXT? A YEAR ON

And, always, time rolls on.

Eddie is the eighteenth Duke of Norfolk, one of a line of holders of this title and stewards of this patch of land dating all the way back to 1138. It is impossible for him not to be aware that, whatever he does here, it is but one small act in the grand sweep of time, and it is what happens after he has gone, and his short tenure is finished, that will keep defining the place, generation after generation.

His son, Henry, knows this as well. His life and career for the last decade have been conducted far from the battlements of Arundel Castle, but he has always kept a practical interest in the estate and its trajectory, as he knows that one day it will be his responsibility. The changes that have been made over the last twenty years – changes that he first started watching as a fourteen-year-old boy – are ones that he feels completely invested in.

'I'm not my father,' he says, 'and we are all motivated by different things in our lives. I probably can't be expected to be as driven, or as single-minded, as he has been over the renaturing of Peppering, but neither can I possibly let it stop here or do anything that sends it backwards.' And he points out that the responsibilities of the estate extend far beyond the farm and the partridge shoot, so his attention will need to be everywhere.

'I was wandering around the woods as a young boy with my

father, learning what was what. For me, it was never only about the shooting, but the whole cocktail of things that went along with it: the beaters, the dogs, the spectacle and the camaraderie. It took time, but eventually I also came to understand the extraordinary achievement of everyone who had been involved, to take what had basically been a prairie and turn it into all this.'

Just as it is important to Henry that he has continually watched the project develop over the years, so it is important to the estate that he has done other things with his life, that he has had a career outside the Arundel bubble. He will bring to it his own stamp.

'What has happened here', he goes on, 'possibly touches the sides of what can make the world a better place. The lessons learned, the mistakes we've made and the biodiversity that has come flooding back – these are all things that can inform a wider debate far away from here. My father may have had the resources to do it in the first place, and the land to demonstrate it on a reasonable scale. But the idea that you can farm for nature, and provide corridors of wildlife that link with hundreds of other farms that may be far smaller, is a really exciting and important one, in the context of a country struggling with its relationship with nature. How could I ever not continue with it?'

But Henry also sees the world through the prism of younger eyes, with different sets of issues and inputs that stretch maybe thirty or forty years ahead. The debate on field sports is generally one that generates more heat than light, even more so now that so much of it has moved into the safe anonymity of social media. He thinks the biggest threat to the continuation of the sport is apathy.

'It was the idea of seeing wild partridges flying once again over the Sussex Downs that started all this,' he says. 'And while it might be convenient to pretend otherwise, it was always shooting that was the driver. It didn't matter that some years we didn't have the surplus birds to shoot at all, let alone a few days; that was just how nature works. Ultimately, it was Dad's vision of a line of guns waiting for a covey of crafty, swerving, fast-flying partridges that were utterly wild that actually made it happen.'

He is standing at a high point on the estate, coincidentally at exactly the point where Dick Potts was standing those twenty years ago, when he decided to go and tell Eddie what had happened to the remaining greys. Looking back down at the flood plain and the castle beyond, Henry is quiet for a moment.

'This has all happened because a human force of nature has driven it, no matter what the cost. That's great, but surely we need to make farming easy enough for anyone with land to do this kind of thing, irrespective of whether they shoot or not, or whether they have the spare cash to finance this kind of stuff.' He pauses, then adds, 'It has all to be more relevant than just to this place. Places like this need to be only the start.'

One hundred and twenty miles to the north-west, a direct part of that relevance is working its way through the hedgerows and headlands of a farm on the southern edge of the Cotswolds.

The land here is very different from that at Peppering: flatter, gentler and more laced with streams, even if the thin Cotswold brash is as tough a farming medium as the chalk and flint in Sussex.

Back in 2016, motivated by nothing more complicated than trying to bring a viable population of grey partridges back to the farm, owner George Ponsonby put an advertisement in the shooting press asking if there was any potential partner wanting to come in with him, with the aim of creating a small wild shoot. The important by-product would, of course, be enough restored nature to stake a reasonable claim to be a 'jewel in the Cotswolds'. No such partner raised their hand, but instead one of Charlie's three beat keepers of the time, Frank Snudden, happened to notice the advertisement and wrote to George asking for his potential services to be taken into account, should the adventure ever happen.

'It ticked so many boxes for me,' he said later. 'It would bring me and my young family back to my home territory, for a start, and it would give me the chance of starting from a blank canvas as the head keeper of a new, small, wild shoot. Keepers don't get that sort of opportunity too often.' He had started his keepering life on a small pheasant shoot, but, like Charlie a decade before, had since been utterly absorbed by the challenges of managing the habitat for greys.

Frank saw out his last season at Peppering, having handed in his notice, and duly arrived at Great Lemhill Farm in March 2017, armed with what he had learned from Charlie and Andrew and the innate knowledge of the countryside that he had immersed himself in as a boy. On the plus side, he quickly saw that the farm had plenty of potential, with large, high hedges, free draining and extensive fields that were perfect for beetle banks. Against that, there were only seventeen pairs of greys when he did his spring counts, which was a pretty precarious genetic baseline from which to grow.

As at Peppering, Frank worked positively alongside the farming operation (including changing the stewardship schemes), creating a series of twelve large beetle banks and getting to grips with the predator control. Within a year he was up to twenty-six pairs on the spring count, which became 226 individual birds by the time he counted again on the autumn stubble. By November, he and George were confident enough to organise a small shooting day of mainly wild pheasants and red-legs, the first day that wild partridges had been driven over guns for more than half a century. The bag that day contained two greys, which went up to twenty-nine the following November, by which time the autumn stubble-counts were showing another near-doubling of birds. Since then the numbers have continued steadily upwards, but the shooting days have deliberately remained small and old-fashioned. And, as at Peppering, the wildlife dividend has been rapid and abundant: yellowhammers, linnets, corn buntings, kestrels, bees and a multitude of butterflies.

'You have created something so special there,' said one of the recent guests in his thank-you letter, 'and I hope that you feel a glowing pride when it all comes right like that.' 'A day I never thought I would experience again,' said another.

The bird numbers have gone up beyond anyone's early expectations, but the shoots have remained small – only the surplus above what can naturally be held by land like that. And, just as Charlie seems to get every keeper of greys in the country to come and help him flanking and turning the birds on his own shoot days, so he and the other members of the Peppering team go over to Great Lemhill each year to return the compliment.

'One thing I never struggle with', says Frank with a smile, 'is numbers for my beating line.'

When asked what were the key attributes that he brought north from Peppering with him, he replies, 'Habitat management, plus stewardship and attention to detail.' He thinks about it a bit more as a covey of nine greys bolt back into the nearby beetle bank and then adds, 'But above all, it's just not messing about with the birds, and instead allowing them to do what they do naturally. That's all we do, really.'

He might have added to that list the importance of having an employer who really would go to the ends of the Earth to make that small dream happen, often in defiance of far easier options. Maybe Frank will one day train up a beat keeper who will carry the same dream somewhere else.

'Everyone has a plan,' as boxer Mike Tyson once said, 'until they get punched in the mouth.' And at dawn a few days later, Charlie is sitting in his Land Rover staring out through a thermal imager into the blood-red sunrise of an empty field, not quite believing what he is seeing. Or, to be more accurate, what he is *not* seeing.

The faint aniseed smell of fennel drifts out of the adjacent wild-flower mix through the half-light and into his open window. Out there, dotted all over the stubble, are the tell-tale heat-signatures of hares and, occasionally, the smaller ones of rabbits. Around the edges and headlands stands the odd covey[1] of pheasants, maybe a wild hen and her five maturing chicks. Little dots in the hedges disclose where the songbirds have roosted for the night and are stirring, all pulses of life that draw the curtain on another day out on the hill. He is seeing many things out there, but what he is not seeing are wild grey partridges.

This is the third day of two weeks of stubble-counts for the team, twelve mornings of getting up before dawn and methodically working their way around each individual field and seeing what is there. From months of observation, they know the number of broods, so it is now merely a question of working out the average surviving brood size and then dividing the first figure by the second and reaching a rough figure for the total number of greys. Partridges don't wander far, so Charlie tends to know which individual covey he is looking at, which helps him not to double-count, which would result in an over-optimistic assessment. And he has done this so often, for so many years, that he can easily tell the heat-signature of the slightly larger red-legged partridge, as much by how it behaves as what it looks like. Once he has spotted a covey of greys, he focuses on them with his powerful binoculars and notes whether they are a pair and their chicks, which is good, or a number of older birds come together, which probably indicates failed breeders and, anyway, doesn't contribute to the overall figure.

Although conditions this year have been excellent, especially with the all-important dry early June, he and the team have been half expecting a bad count. After all, they are out on the ground for most of the day, every day, and they cannot fail to register – even if subconsciously – whether they are coming across more birds, or fewer birds, than in previous years. In a way, all that is happening on this cool Friday morning is confirmation of what everyone has already been thinking: that some uncontrollable factor has taken hold this year.

Over the last few days Charlie has asked himself on more than one occasion, 'What would Dick Potts say?', wishing, for reasons beyond his obvious deep friendship with the man, that Dick was around professionally to help him put it all into context. He is pretty sure that Dick would say, 'It's nature, Charlie. You can do many things to help it along, but you are never going to control it.'

Down on the farm, they think it might be the rats, which have benefited explosively from the dry conditions, but the team have been at them, relentlessly, every day of the season. Kate thinks it might be the drought, and that maybe the extreme heat of late July and early August was too much for young birds, even when sheltering under a hedge or in some thick cover. Charlie himself wonders whether it might be some undetected illness or, of greater concern, a weakening of the gene pool of what is, in effect, just a small island population of a species that has died out everywhere around. Dick had more than once quoted the great biologist E. O. Wilson about the fragility of island populations and how it was that, the smaller the island, the more fragile its biodiversity was.

Peppering would only ever truly thrive inasmuch as the local area allowed it to, because the nature of wildlife is not to be static but to move and not want to be penned into a couple of thousand hectares. Besides, it was only a hundred years ago that head keepers from the country's greatest partridge manors would converge on King's Cross Station on a specific day in May, equipped with special belts that kept the eggs they contained at body temperature, and swap those eggs with other keepers to freshen up the gene pool. Some would end up going to different corners of their own estates, some to nearby places and others to the far end of the country. Wherever they went, the effect was to keep the national population in peak genetic health.

Charlie drives on, knowing that he only has about seventy-five minutes before daylight brings out the buzzards and kites, at which point any small game bird will disappear smartly from the open stubble and back into cover. Occasionally he finds a good strong covey, maybe a hen and a cock with nine young but, more generally, field after field disappoints. As he drives back to his cottage for breakfast, he thinks about his boss. The Duke enables all this to happen, and Charlie has an uncomplicated desire to reward his commitment with a couple of good days for him and his friends and other paying guests. Equally, those days are among the most important in the year for around eighty other people, so it matters.

Then he thinks about Dick Potts again. '2012', he had pointed out to Charlie and the team more than once, 'was the wettest summer, and the worst partridge year we ever had. But what happened next?'

Charlie well remembered what had happened next: 2014 had been the best year in Peppering's history.

In the early days of September, and as the recent stubble-count is rationalised into being one of the many caprices of nature, Charlie and Kate host a pre-season barbecue in their garden for the team. The swifts have already left from under the eaves for their long journey to Africa, but it is still high summer up here and there is warmth in the setting sun.

It's a team that has grown organically over the years, and comes from all corners of the locality: the beat keepers are there with their partners, dressed for once in jeans and T-shirts rather than their green and grey working clothes. The beaters come along as well, as do the picking-up team, the game-cart drivers, the digger operators and the whole human fabric that keeps this enterprise going, year on year, under the surface. Small children seem to be underfoot everywhere, and even the local game-dealer has turned from customer into supplier and produced the burgers and steaks for the barbecue. Straw bales supplement the few trestle tables and chairs, and it seems that just about every stick of furniture has been dragged out of the cottage to produce sitting room for the sixty or seventy people who have come along. Cans of beer and Coke are crammed into black dustbins full of icy water, and out of the open windows of the shepherd's hut that normally doubles as Charlie's office comes the sound of an eclectic playlist made especially for the evening by Kate, on which 'Summer of '69' rubs shoulders with the *Peter Rabbit* theme tune.

The Return of the Grey Partridge

Not everyone has made it. Some are up north with Eddie on the grouse moors, others on holiday. As with any gathering, the strange summer of war in Ukraine, the cost-of-living crisis and drought on the Sussex hills has been kinder to some than others, but you can always make out in the rising and falling of the conversation and laughter the uncomplicated contentment of any group of people who have come together socially in a common cause. The talk is of local things: of avian flu and how it is taking a devastating toll on the seabirds on the northern coasts, and of how difficult it has been to get pheasant poults on other local shoots this year; anecdotes of slip-ups and little idiocies from previous seasons send pulses of loud laughter out over the garden. The occasional silence is punctuated by the snap of pigeon wings, as the birds rise up from the wires and soar and dive over the garden and neighbouring fields.

For twenty years now, this entire human ecosystem has evolved around the fortunes of one bird, a half-kilo native of the downland that has been brought back from the brink of local extinction. And everyone in Charlie's garden knows instinctively that what was good for that bird also turned out to be good for the soil and water, the flowers and weeds, the invertebrates and songbirds and, indirectly, the humans who worked alongside it. They know that they are privileged to be part of a culture whose time often seems to be waning in the wider world, and are therefore all the more conscious of their responsibility to protect and enhance it.

Deep down, they also know that they are all simply actors, and Peppering merely the stage, in a single tiny moment of theatre in the vast sweep of the natural history of this corner of England.

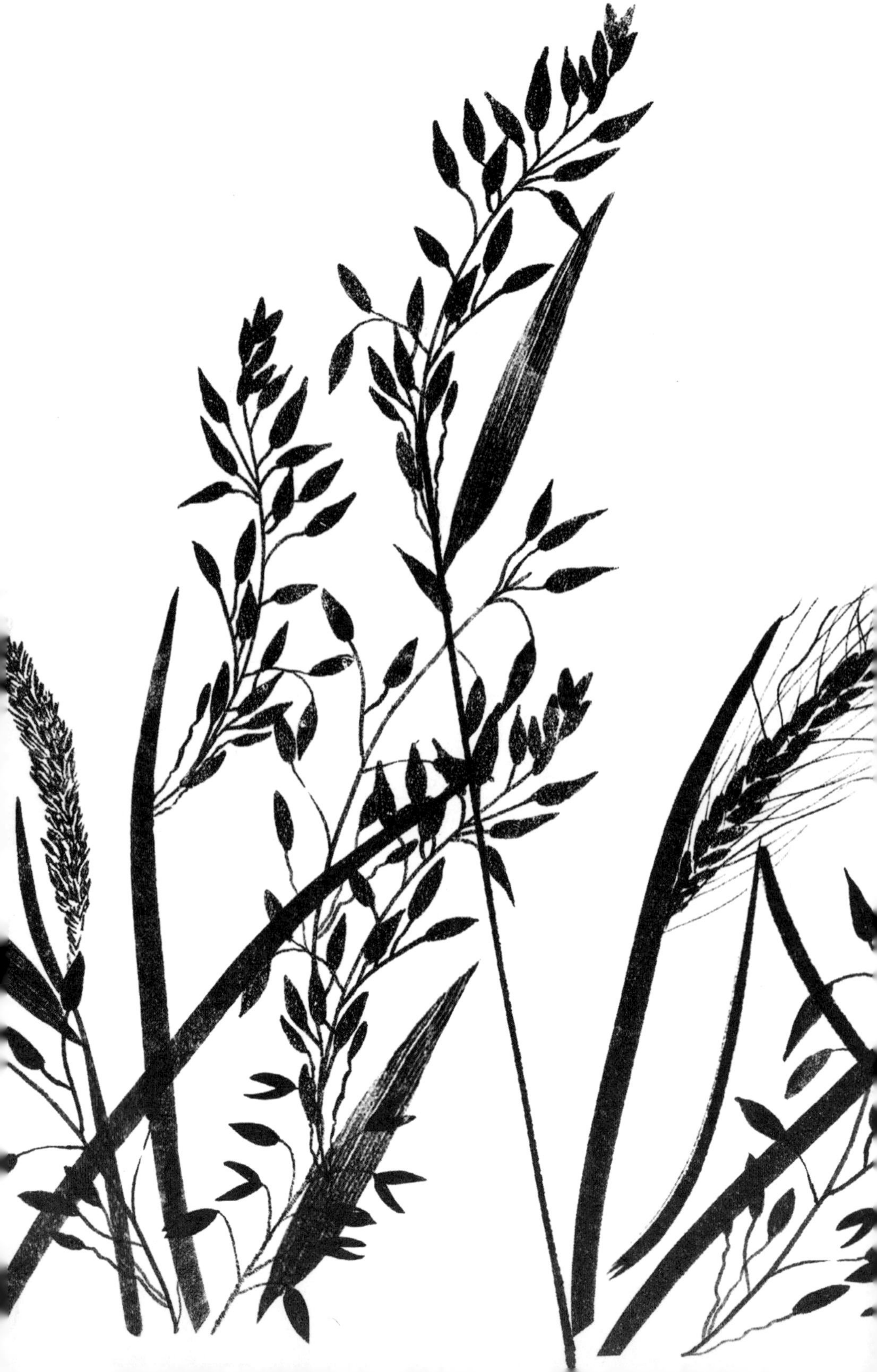

TABLES

Development of grey partridge numbers

Year	Spring pair count (pairs)	September stubble-counts (birds)	Average young per clutch
2003	3	11	(unknown)
2004	11	91	(unknown)
2005	18	150	(unknown)
2006	32	220	(unknown)
2007	45	262	4.6
2008	72	754	9.5
2009	181	1,217	6.7
2010	262	2,150	8.9
2011	337	1,978	5.3
2012	367	860	1.6
2013	252	1,412	5.2
2014	292	2,226	8.2
2015	343	2,011	5.3
2016	320	1,272	3.9
2017	285	1,379	4.5
2018	268	1,308	5.4
2019	234	938	3.9
2020	219	1,156	4.5
2021	272	945	3.2

Note effect of wet June (e.g. 2012).

Important arable wild flower species recorded 2018–2022

Common name	Scientific name	Plantlife score
Corn mint	*Mentha arvensis*	1
Cornfield knotgrass	*Polygonum rurivagum*	3
Dense-flowered fumitory	*Fumaria densiflora*	3
Dwarf spurge	*Euphorbia exigua*	6
Field madder	*Sherardia arvensis*	1
Field woundwort	*Stachys arvensis*	6
Fine-leaved fumitory	*Fumaria parviflora*	7
Henbit deadnettle	*Lamium amplexicaule*	1
Narrow-fruited cornsalad	*Valerianella dentata*	8
Night-flowering catchfly	*Silene noctiflora*	7
Prickly poppy	*Papaver argemone*	7
Rough poppy	*Papaver hybridum*	3
Round-leaved fluellen	*Kickxia spuria*	3
Sharp-leaved fluellen	*Kickxia elatine*	2
Small toadflax	*Chaenorhinum minus*	1
Venus'-looking-glass	*Legousia hybrida*	3

Total insect count at Peppering

	2020	2021	2022	
Records made	1,184	1,247	1,331	
Beetle species identified	140	140	154	
Butterfly species identified	17	17	25	
Species identified	411	425	471	
Accumulated species recorded (2020–2022)				687
Species with conservation status				67
% with conservation status				9.90

Red-listed bird abundance

Species	*Breeding status*	*Breeding evidence*
Corn Bunting	Probable	Holding Territory
Cuckoo	Probable	Holding Territory
Grey Partridge	Confirmed	Fledged young
Herring Gull	Non-breeding	Foraging only
House Sparrow	Confirmed	Fledged young
Lapwing	Confirmed	Young observed
Linnet	Probable	Nest building
Mistle Thrush	Probable	Holding Territory
Skylark	Probable	Holding Territory
Song Thrush	Probable	Holding Territory
Starling	Confirmed	Fledged young
Turtle Dove	Possible	In suitable habitat
Yellowhammer	Probable	Holding Territory

These were observed in formal transects in early June. A further 52 species were observed, of which 11 were from the amber list.

The Return of the Grey Partridge

Development of raptor and owl numbers from 2005–2013

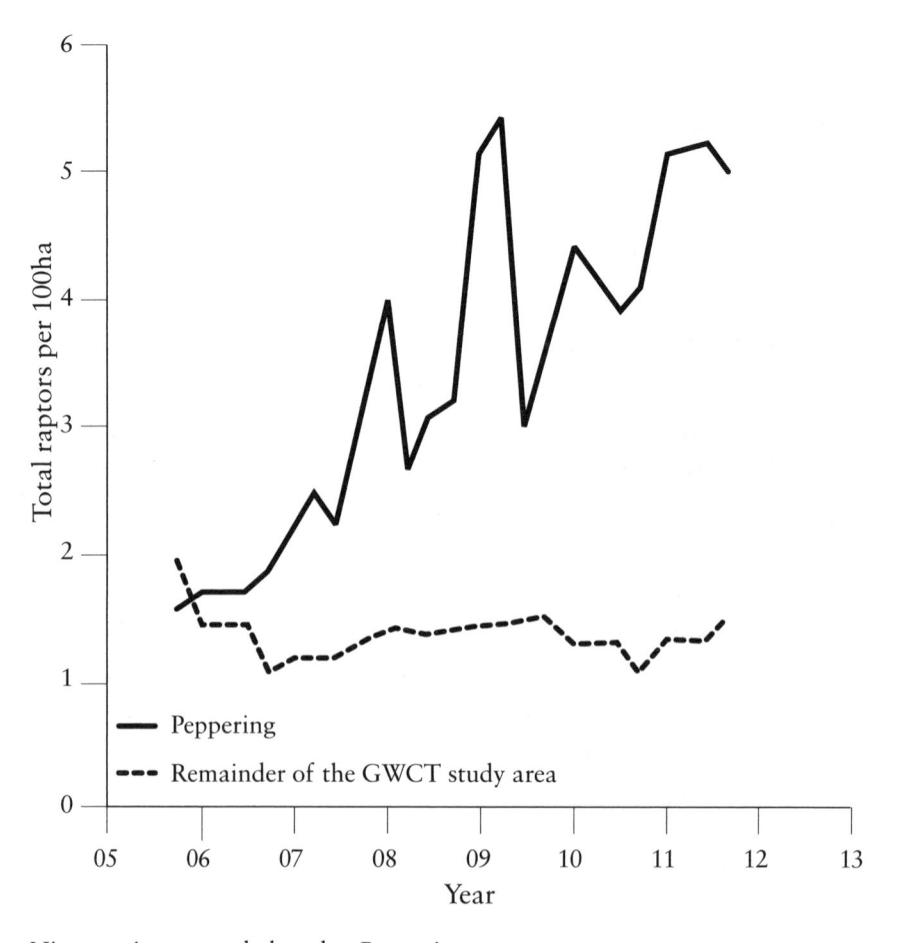

Nine species currently breed at Peppering:

- Buzzard
- Sparrowhawk
- Peregrine
- Kestrel
- Hobby
- Barn Owl
- Tawny Owl
- Little Owl
- Red Kite

NOTES

1. The Circling Storm
1. *Alectoris rufa.*
2. More recent surveys in Finland have confirmed this, noting that the population of forest grouse that are normally harried by foxes has burgeoned after the reintroduction of the fox-hunting lynx.
3. *Alectoris chukar.*
4. The Zanclean flood, which is thought to have refilled the Mediterranean Sea about 5 million years ago, was so rapid that at times the water depth increased by ten metres a day.
5. In 2020 this figure stood at around 3,000 (National Gamekeepers' Organisation).
6. *ShootingUK* article (4 August 2014).
7. 'When everything changed: the US and UK economies in World War 2', Rapid Transition Alliance (25 June 2019).
8. It is rarely mentioned in the history books that the effect of what was an 11 per cent decline in food consumption was almost entirely beneficial. Such obesity as there was, infant mortality and the suicide rate all showed marked declines.
9. Graham Harvey, *Grass-Fed Nation: Getting Back the Food We Deserve* (Icon Books, 2016).
10. Alexandre Antonelli, *The Hidden Universe: Adventures in Biodiversity* (Witness Books, 2022).

11 The South Downs Way itself was opened as a long-distance footpath in July 1972.
12 R. A. Robinson and W. J. Sutherland, 'Post-war changes in arable farming and biodiversity in Great Britain', *Journal of Applied Ecology* (June 2002).
13 Somewhere between 35 and 60 million pheasants are now released each year, of which around 40 per cent might get shot. This gives rise to the curious phenomenon that, on any October day, not far off half of the avian biomass of the UK consists of just the one bird species.
14 Conway and Petty (1990).
15 Rachel Carson, *Silent Spring* (Houghton Mifflin, 1962).
16 R. E. A. Almond et al. (eds), *Living Planet Report 2020: Bending the Curve of Biodiversity Loss* (WWF, 2020).
17 Tris Allinson et al. (eds), *State of the World's Birds: Taking the Pulse of the Planet* (BirdLife International, 2018).

2. The Three-Legged Stool

1 S. J. Harris et al., *The Breeding Bird Survey 2019: Population Trends of the UK's Breeding Birds* (British Trust for Ornithology, 2020).
2 Simon J. Butler et al., 'An objective, niche-based approach to indicator species selection', *Methods in Ecology and Evolution* (January 2012).
3 Jake Fiennes, *Land Healer: How Farming Can Save Britain's Countryside* (Witness Books, 2022).
4 In 2021 this figure was more like 85 per cent.
5 A figure generally agreed to be around twenty pairs per 100 hectares.

3. Beetle Banks and Buzzards

1 A pen-picture for which I am indebted to Peppering's consultant ornithologist, Richard Black.
2 A hand-operated broadcast seeder that was carried against the

Notes

farmer's chest and used an action like playing a fiddle to get the seed out of the bag and onto the ground. It was reckoned that a man could sow almost a hectare an hour with one.

4. A Special Delivery
1. Dick only counted plants that were UK Biodiversity Action Plan species.

5. Forty Years On
1. The full list was: sparrowhawk, hen harrier, peregrine, other raptor, fence collision, fox, dog, Fenn trap, farm machinery and illness.
2. Natural England is the body established within DEFRA to ensure that England's natural capital (for example, flora, fauna, fresh water, coastal areas, geology and soils) is protected and improved, and that people are enabled to enjoy, understand and access the natural environment. It was formed in 2006, coincidentally the same year that Peppering was taken back in hand.
3. 'Number of pet dogs in the UK', 2021/22 figures, statista.com.
4. Libby Field's long life came to an end in the winter of 2022–3, between the writing and the publication of this book, bringing to a close many decades of close involvement with the estate.

7. Predator Control
1. The wet early summer of 2012, for example, put a cart and horses through the hatching season, and it was decided in consequence that there would be no shooting at all that season.
2. A trophic cascade occurs when apex predators, in controlling the mesopredators below them, come to beneficially affect the survival rates of the layers of life below. Or vice versa.
3. D. W. Gibbons et al., 'The predation of wild birds in the UK', RSPB Research Report, 2007.

4   As opposed to illegal predator control, better known as 'persecution', which is exactly that: illegal.
5   Game & Wildlife Conservation Trust research paper.
6   'Carrion crow', BirdFacts, British Trust for Ornithology, bto.org.
7   A Larsen trap is a simple wire box with two chambers, in one of which sits a decoy bird, whose role is to attract territorial local corvids in, which then can't leave.

8. The Scientists
1   Stephen Moss, 'Obituary: Dick Potts', *Guardian*, 4 May 2017.
2   Herpetologists, mycologists, ichthyologists and lepidopterists are specialists in reptiles/amphibians, fungi, fish biology and butterflies/moths respectively.
3   A year on, this figure is now above 600.
4   Requiring higher temperatures for normal development.
5   The British Trust for Ornithology publishes a regular list of Birds of Conservation Concern, into whose 2021 endangered Red List category the lapwing has been placed, along with the grey partridge, corn bunting, hen harrier, linnet, skylark and yellowhammer.
6   A British food-quality assurance certification programme.

9. Curlews
1   Disclosure: the author, being chair of the conservation charity Curlew Action, may be more animated on this subject than on others.
2   www.curlewaction.org
3   Courts are now handing down prison sentences for any unauthorised removal of the eggs of Red-Listed birds, which include curlews.
4   The slight cracking of the shell that is carried out by the chick inside and precedes hatching.
5   In the interests of full disclosure, in the closing months of

his life Dick Potts had emboldened Charlie to try exactly this sort of non-partridge-related adventure, so maybe he knew all along.

10. The Soil Underneath

1. Strictly speaking, wild animals that weigh more than forty kilos.
2. Paul Jepson and Cain Blythe, *Rewilding: The Radical New Science of Ecological Recovery* (Icon Books, 2020).
3. www.groundswellag.com
4. The characteristic of breaking easily into smaller pieces under pressure.

11. Dwellers All in Time and Space

1. J. A. Ewald et al., 'Investigation of the impact of changes in pesticide use on invertebrate populations', Natural England Commissioned Report, NECR182, 2016.
2. 'Arun to Adur Farmer's Group', Farmer Clusters, farmerclusters.com.
3. Alexandre Antonelli, *The Hidden Universe* (Witness Books, 2022).
4. Hawthorn, blackthorn, hazel, field maple, spindle, gelder rose, holly, privet, dogwood and dog rose.
5. Cocksfoot, tall fescue, slender creeping red fescue and timothy.
6. Yarrow, agrimony, kidney vetch, betany, common knapweed, greater knapweed, dropwort, hedge bedstraw, lady's bedstraw, horseshoe vetch, rough hawkbit, oxeye daisy, bird's-foot trefoil, wild marjoram, ribwort plantain, salad burnet, cowslip, selfheal, meadow buttercup, common sorrel, small scabious, bladder campion, tufted vetch, quaking grass, glaucous sedge, crested dog's-tail, sheep's fescue, red fescue, crested hair-grass, smaller cat's-tail, yellow oat-grass.

12. Lee Farm: Mid-Autumn

1   Robert H. MacArthur and Edward O. Wilson, *The Theory of Island Biogeography* (Princeton University Press, 1967).

13. Shoot Day

1   In researching this book, it is hard to overexaggerate the sadness that the cutting short of Dick's life has had on the wider 'partridge community', although Dick did live to see his project reach fruition.

14. Where Next?

1   Covey is a collective noun for pheasants as well as for partridges. Other collective nouns for pheasants are bouquet, nye, head, nide, nest and flock.

BIBLIOGRAPHY

James Aldred, *Goshawk Summer: The Diary of an Extraordinary Season in the Forest* (Elliott & Thompson, 2021)
Alexandre Antonelli, *The Hidden Universe: Adventures in Biodiversity* (Witness Books, 2022)
James Canton, *The Oak Papers* (Canongate Books, 2020)
Mark Cocker, *Our Place: Can We Save Britain's Wildlife Before It Is Too Late?* (Vintage, 2018)
Tim Dee, *Greenery: Journeys in Springtime* (Penguin, 2020)
Roy Dennis, *Restoring the Wild: Sixty Years of Rewilding Our Skies, Woods and Waterways* (William Collins, 2021)
Dan Eatherley, *Invasive Aliens: Plants and Animals from Over There That Are Over Here* (William Collins, 2020)
Jake Fiennes, *Land Healer: How Farming Can Save Britain's Countryside* (Witness Books, 2022)
Thor Hanson, *Hurricane Lizards and Plastic Squid: The Fraught and Fascinating Biology of Climate Change* (Icon Books, 2022)
Sophie Lake et al., *Britain's Habitats: A Field Guide to the Wildlife Habitats of Great Britain and Ireland* (Princeton Press, 2015)
Philip Lymbery, *Sixty Harvests Left: How to Reach a Nature-friendly Future* (Bloomsbury, 2022)

James Macdonald Lockhart, *Raptor: A Journey Through Birds* (Fourth Estate, 2016)

Benedict Macdonald, *Cornerstones: Wild Forces That Can Change Our World* (Bloomsbury Wildlife, 2022)

Benedict MacDonald, *Rebirding: Restoring Britain's Wildlife* (Pelagic Publishing, 2019)

Andrew Painting, *Regeneration: The Rescue of a Wild Land* (Birlinn, 2021)

G. R. (Dick) Potts, *Partridges* (Collins, 2012)

Enric Sala, *The Nature of Nature: Why We Need the Wild* (National Geographic, 2020)

Joe Schute, *Forecast: A Diary of the Lost Seasons* (Bloomsbury Wildlife, 2021)

ACKNOWLEDGEMENTS

Henry Arundel
Jack Barton
Ryan Burrell
Dom Buscall
Caroline Clark
David Clarke
Mary Colwell
Edward Darling
Julie Ewald
Libby Field
Nick Field
Jake Fiennes
Mark Firth
Rick Goring
Conor Haydon
Andrew Hoodless
Adam Huttly
Peter Jones
Sue Kennard
Peter Knight
Charlie Mellor
Kate Mellor
Caroline Morgan-Grenville
Chris North
Lloyd Park
Martin Pimm
George Ponsonby
Olga Potts
Ellie Rivers
Frank Snudden
Andrew Stringer
Mark Watson
Beauford Witney
Niall Wright

PICTURE CREDITS

p. xix Distribution map: reprinted by permission of *Fieldsports*

Plate section

2: Roger Morgan-Grenville; 3: Roger Morgan-Grenville; 4: FLPA / Alamy Stock Photo; 5 top: Adam Huttly; 5 bottom: Roger Morgan-Grenville; 6, 7, 8, 9 top: Adam Huttly; 9 bottom: Premaphotos / Alamy Stock Photo; 10 top: mauritius images GmbH / Alamy Stock Photo; 10 bottom: Roger Morgan-Grenville; 11: Roger Morgan-Grenville; 12 top: Adam Huttly; 12 bottom: Roger Morgan-Grenville; 13: Roger Morgan-Grenville; 14, 15: Mark Firth; 16 top: Mark Firth

INDEX

Page numbers in **bold** refer to tables; page numbers preceded by 'P' refer to the colour illustration section.

academic research projects 131–4
agriculture
  biodiversity/farming balance
    63–75
  catchment ground
    management 72–3, 121, 131
  cattle 71, 119–20
  commodity prices 74
  Common Agricultural Policy 9
  decline of bird species on
    farmland 27, 97
  during Second World War 7
  fertiliser use 118
  and game bird shooting 64, 68
  habitat loss and species decline
    7–8, 27, 97, 134
  harvesting, timing of 22
  herbicide and insecticide use
    9–10, 91
  intensive farming xxiv–xxvi, 9
  natural pollination failure x
  patchwork-quilt farming
    viii, P1, 21, 31, 38 43, 63
  pesticide use 9–10, 123
  pigs 71, 118-9
  post-1945 7–11
  prairie farming 8
  Red Tractor certification 100
  regenerative farming 68, 75,
    116, 121–2
  and renaturing 115–16
  rotation farming 64–5, 139
  sheep farming 24, 65, 68–71,
    118, 120, 139
  stewardship schemes 32, 47–8,
    66, 72, 74, 139
  subsidies 7, 8, 47
  and tidiness 100
  see also North Stoke Farm,
    biodiversity project; soil
    management
'angel wings' 108–9
'Anthropocene' 4, 14 88
apex predators 4, 6, 14, 48 77–9,
  114
arable flora surveys 92–3, **172**
Arkengarthdale, North Yorkshire
  101, 105

Index

Arun to Adur Farmer's Group 128–31
ash dieback disease 96
Avery, Mark 127

badgers 24, 81, 84, 128, 155
barbecue party 167–8
barley production 31, 65
beat keepers 25, 33, 37-8, 51, 52, 56, 66, 68, 71, 85, 87–8, 100, 103, 138, 144-5, 147, 164, 166, 169
beaters 52, 54, 71, 125, 148, 150-1, 153-6, 162
beavers 78
beetle banks P2, 18, 21, 28–9, 40, 46
  construction of 29, 141–2
  hedging 30, 39
biodiversity
  farm 'clusters' 89
  global decline in 11
  of Peppering Estate xviii
  pesticide use impact 9
  see also North Stoke Farm, biodiversity project; Peppering Partridge Project
bird species
  abundance of in early 19th-century 26
  breeding strategies 144
  decline of on farmland 27, 97
  global decline in 11
  increase in number of 40–1
  Red-Listed species 96, 97, 133
  satellite-tracking 104, 109–10, 111
  surveys of 95–8
  use of feeders 40
  see also individual species
birds of prey *see* raptors
Black, Rich 95–8, 99
botanical surveys 92–3, **172**
Britain, food imports 7
bullfinches 99
Burrell, Ryan 97, 132–4
butterflies P5, 131, **173**
buzzards 96

capital grants 48
Carson, Rachel 9
catchment ground management 72–3, 121, 131
cats, feral 81-3
cattle 71, 119–20
Charles II 5
chukar partridges 5
Clark, David 36–7
clay-shooting 20
climate change 11, 95
commodity prices 74
Common Agricultural Policy 9
community outreach work 125–31
conservation
  head-starting process 103–4
  key areas 91–2
  planning meetings 98–100
conservation headlands 22, 48–9, 92
corn buntings viii, xxv, xvii, P5, 26, 87, 97, 99, 133
corn salad 92
corvids 79, 81

control of 83, 86–7
Countryside Stewardship (CS)
　scheme 32, 139
cows 119–20
crows *see* corvids
curlew project P7, 101–12, 128
　chick-rearing 107–8
　financing of 105, 112
　head-starting process 103–4
　incubation and hatching of
　　eggs 106
　outdoor rearing pens 108–9
　release pens 110–11
　satellite-tagging 109–10, 111
　sourcing of eggs 105
curlews
　as an indicator species 102
　decline in number of 101

DDT 10, 91, 99
deer 24, 35, 67, 80, 84
dewponds 33, 121
dog-owners, irresponsible
　behaviour of 48
dogs
　as wildlife threat 22, 24, 48, 82
　working dogs on shoot day P9,
　　154
Duke of Burgundy butterfly
　130-1
Dunkirk evacuation (1940) xv

ecosystems, man's disturbance
　of 113
EEC 9
electric fences 80
elk 77–8

Entry Level Stewardship (ELS)
　scheme 47
Ewald, Julie xxi–xxii, 123–5
extinctions xii, 14

farm 'clusters', biodiversity
　projects 89
farm visits 126–8
farming *see* agriculture
feeders 22, 34, 40, 42
fencing
　along footpaths 22
　capital grants for 48
　electric fences 80
　hedge protection 24
fertiliser use 118
Field, Libby 53–4
Field, Nick 27–9, 31, 32, 46, 52-3,
　69, 139, 140–3
field size, reduction of 18
field voles 3, 76
Fiennes, Jake 16
finches vii, 27, 41, 99
First World War 6
Fitzalan-Howard, Edward,
　18th Duke of Norfolk (Eddie
　Norfolk) P9
　approach to conservation 102,
　　125, 135
　curlew project 102–3, 105, 106,
　　111
　grey partridge shooting xiii,
　　50–6, 151
　head keeper appointment 57
　Lee Farm, taken back in hand
　　136–7
　origin of renaturing project

xxiii–xxvii
Purdey Awards for Game and Conservation 57–9
Fitzalan-Howard, Henry, Earl of Arundel 161-63
Fitzalan-Howard, Miles, 17th Duke of Norfolk, wartime experiences xiii–xvi
flankers 52, 53, 151, 153
flint 139, 140, 142
footpaths 22, 140, 142
foxes 81–2, 133
  control of P6, 84
fumitory 92
funding schemes *see* stewardship schemes

game bird shooting
  appeal and benefits of xvii–xviii, 127
  Eddie Norfolk's first shoot xiii
  genetic health of birds 166
  grey partridge shooting P8, 50–6, 143–55
  history of 145
  integration with farming practices 64, 68
  knowledge of grey partridge behaviour 146, 149
  and land management practice 17
  lunch for shooting party 53, 54
  as a 'numbers game' 54–6, 145
  pheasant shooting 20, 21, 51
  pickers-up P9, 154
  preparation for shoot day 146, 147
  public debate/engagement 125, 160–1
  shoot day 143–55
  shootable surplus 23, 143, 144
  star-burst display, airborne birds P8, 153
  'turning' the bird 52
  wild pheasant shooting 67
  wildlife benefits of xvii–xviii, 127
Game and Wildlife Conservation Trust (GWCT) x, 30, 90, 92
gamekeepers 6, 33, 146–7
  see also beat keepers; Mellor, Charlie; Snudden, Frank; Stringer, Andrew
godwits 104
Goodridge, Tom 51, 52
Goring, Rick 131
goshawks 147–8
government
  and habitat/species decline xi–xviii
grain feeders 22, 40, 42
Great Lemhill Farm 164-5
Great War 6
'green manure' 117–18
grey partridges
  artificial rearing of 5
  chick loss to predation 81
  and climate change 11
  clutch size P3, 19, **171**
  decline in number of xiii–xiv, xxi–xxvi, 6, 11, 97, 164–6, **171**
  displacement of into neighbouring land 45–6

189

egg laying 19
egg loss to predation 80–1
evolution of 4
gifting of from Peppering Estate to other estates in southern England 43–4
GWCT count on South Downs xix
increase in number of P3, x, xvii, 40, 42, 57–8, 171
as indicator species xxvi, 15
insect food preferences 19
knowledge of partridge behaviour 146, 149
predation of 45, 80–3
protection from dogs 22
relocation of birds from Sandringham to Arundel Estate 36–41
spring pair counts 171
stubble-counts xxi–xxvi, 123–4, 163, 164–6, 171
'three-legged stool' model 12, 13–25, 34, 49
and weather conditions 171
see also game bird shooting

grey squirrels 80
grit 22–3
ground-nesting birds
  hedgerow habitat 30
  increase in number of 43
  predation of 71, 80–3
GWCT *see* Game and Wildlife Conservation Trust

habitat loss xii, 7–8, 27, 134

hares P5, 34, 152
harvesting, timing of 22
Haydon, Conor 63–9, 71–2, 73, 74, 100, 129, 130
  Lee Farm, taken back in hand 137, 138–40
  regenerative farming 121–2
  soil improvement 116–18
head-starting process, curlew project 103–4
headland strips 22, 48–9, 92
hedgehogs 80
hedgerows P1, 29, 30–1, 38–9, 46
  capital grants for hedging 48
  cutting of 134
  fence protection 24
  grass margins alongside 134–5
  laying of P2, 134
  microclimates of 98, 134
  plant species in vicinity of 135
  ponds adjacent to 99
  removal of 7, 8
  strip cover 18–19
  thickening of 99
  tree species used in 30
Hedley, Colin 92–5, 100, 129
hen harriers P4
Henry III 5
herbicide use 9
Higher Level Stewardship (HLS) scheme 32, 47, 139
Holkham, Norfolk 99
Home Farm xxv, 16, 27, 30, 42, 46, 51, 95
human population, growth of xii, 11, 14

Index

indicator species 15, 102
insecticide use 9–10, 91
insects xi, P5, P7, 19
  biodiversity increase 76, 94, 95, 100
  invertebrate surveys 94–5, **173**
Italian campaign (Second World War) xvi–xvii

jays 83

kale strips 43
kestrels 154
Knight, Peter xxiii–iv 15–21, 24, 28, 31, 32, 46, 47, 52, 57–9, 80, 90-1, 125, 128, 142
  beetle banks 28–9
  conservation priorities 91–2
  eulogy for Dick Potts 90–1
  grey partridge shooting 52
  outreach work 128
knotgrass beetles 11

lambing time 69, 70
land-sparing (set-aside land) 17, 40–1
lapwings P7, 74, 90–1, 97, 132–3
Larsen trap 86–8
Lee Farm 136–42
  beetle bank construction 141–2
  cropping plan 139
  'Dog Leg' 140
  flint clearance 139
linnets P4, 40, 43
livestock farming 71, 118–20
  see also sheep farming
Locke, David 20
Lyons, Graeme ix, P7, 93–5, 100 134

MacDonald, Alex 47-8
manure 71–2, 117–18
'Meet the farmer' project 130–1
Mellor, Charlie P7, 33, 56, 57, 63–9, 73, 81-2, 85-7, 91-2, 95, 100, 103, 106-8, 110-1, 115, 122
  barbecue party for estate team 167–8
  conservation priorities 91–2
  curlew project 103, 106, 107, 108, 111
  Lee Farm taken back in hand 137
  predator control 81, 82, 83, 85–6
  shoot day 143–55
  stubble-counts 164–6
Mellor, Kate 107, 166, 167–8
'mesopredators' 78–9
Military Cross, awarded to Miles Fitzalan-Howard xvi–xvii
moles 81
Muir, John xxv

National Farmers' Union (NFU) 7
Natural England 32–3, 47, 49, 105, 112, 126, 129
neonicotinoids 10
nest boxes 88
nest-cams 24
night-vision devices 86, 124

nightingales 99
nitrogen-fixing plants 117–18
Norfolk, Eddie *see* Fitzalan-Howard, Edward...
Norman, Roy 37
North Stoke Farm, biodiversity project 17–19
  beetle banks 28–9
  displacement of grey partridges into neighbouring land 45–6
  field size reduction 18
  funding schemes 32
  hedgerows and strip cover 18–19
  increase in grey partridge numbers 40, 42
  predation of grey partridges 45
  principles of 33–4
  team members 31–2
Northumberland, Duke of 58

oilseed rape 43, 65
Oostvaardersplassen, Netherlands 114
otters 99
owls P4, 40, 81, 88, 96

partridges
  evolution of 4–5
  genetic health of birds 166
  hunting of 4, 5
  predation of 45, 79, 80–3
  see also game bird shooting; grey partridges
peas 31, 63, 65, 74
Peppering Estate
  biodiversity of xvii
  bird species xvii
  curlew project 101–12, 128
  farm visits 126–8
  gifting of grey partridges to other estates 43–4
  Lee Farm taken back in hand 136–42
  North Stoke and Peppering Farms taken back in hand 17, 46
  'Peppering C' study site 132
  scientific research projects 131–4
  wild grey partridge count **xix**
  see also game bird shooting
Peppering Farm
  biodiversity project 17–19
  prairie farming 8
  taken back in hand 17, 46
Peppering Partridge Project xvi-i 46–50
  agricultural operations 49, 63–75
  biodiversity surveys 89, 92–8, **172**, **173**
  biodiversity/farming balance 63–75
  bird surveys 95–8
  botanical surveys 92–3, **172**
  catchment ground management 72–3, 121, 131
  community outreach work 125–31
  conservation planning meetings 98–100
  conservation priorities 91–2

Index

invertebrate surveys 94–5, **173**
North Stoke and Peppering Farms taken back in hand 17, 46
public education/engagement 125–31
sheep farming, role of 68–71
stewardship schemes 32, 47–8, 66, 72, 74, 139
see also game bird shooting; North Stoke Farm, biodiversity project
pesticide use 9–10, 123
pheasants
 game shooting 20, 21, 51, 67
 predation of 9, 79
 threat posed by neighbouring reared birds 34
 use of feeders 42
Philip, Prince, Duke of Edinburgh 36, 41, 55
pickers-up, shoot day 154
pig manure 71–2, 117
pigs 71, 119
Pimm, Martin 69–71
Pleistocene era 4
poison use, predator control 86
pollination of agricultural crops x
ponds 33, 99, 121
Ponsonby, George 163-5
population growth, human xii, 11, 14
Potts, Dick xii, xiii, xxi–v, P9, 21, 32, 123, 151, 165
 biodiversity increase 76
 biodiversity surveys 89
 climate change and the grey partridge 11
 consultant ecologist appointment 34–5
 decline in grey partridge numbers xiii–xiv, xxiii–xxvi
 and grey partridge shooting 17, 50–1
 hedgerows 30
 illness and death of 90–1
 increase in grey partridge numbers 40
 legacy of 90–1
 pesticide use, biodiversity impact 9
 predation of grey partridges 45
 predator control 80
 relocation of gifted birds from Sandringham to Arundel Estate 36–41
 stubble-counts of grey partridges xxi–xxiii, 123–4, 171
 'three-legged stool' model 12, 13–25, 34, 49
Potts, Olga 91
predator control xviii, xix, 9, 23–5, 80–8, 127–8
 emotiveness of subject 79
 Larsen trap 86–7
 poison 86
 shooting 84, 85
 snares 84, 85
 Tully trap P6
 tunnel traps 83, 85, 87
 work routines of beat keepers

193

87–8
predator numbers, fluctuations in 13
see also apex predators
prey populations 13, 78
Purdey Awards for Game and Conservation 57–9

radio-tagging, of birds 110
Rampion offshore wind farm 73
raptors
    increase in number of P4, 34, 41, 43, 96
    persecution of 26–7
    population collapse 27
    predation of grey partridges 45, 81
    scientific research on 132
rats 67, 82, 166
    control of 80, 84, 85–6
Raveningham Estate, Suffolk 16
ravens 70–1, 83, 96
red-backed shrikes 27
red-legged partridges 4, 5, 26, 34, 40, 81, 108, 150, 154, 167
Red Listed bird species 96, 97, 133
Red Tractor certification 100
regenerative farming 68, 75, 116, 121–2
rewilding 89, 114, 115, 116
Romney sheep 68, 120
rooks 83
rotation farming 64–5, 139
rough poppy P3, 35, 93
RSPB xviii, 127
Ruabon grouse moor xviii–xix

rural culture, and intensive agriculture 8

Sandringham Estate 6, 36–41, 50, 104
satellite-tracking, of birds P7, 104, 109–10, 111
sawflies 10, 19
scientific research projects 131–4
Second World War xv–xvii, 6–7
set-aside land 17, 40–1
sewage sludge 71–2
sheep farming 65, 68–71, 118, 120, 139
    damage to birds' eggs 24
    lambing time 69, 70
shepherds 68–71
shooting of game birds *see* game bird shooting
shooting, predator control 84, 85
signage 33
Simpson, Sue 48, 49
skylarks 40, 76, 97, 98
'slipped wings' 108–9
snakes 80
snares, predator control 84, 85
Snudden, Frank 164-66
soil, downland 64
soil management
    flint clearance 139
    organic content/fertility improvement 115–18
    soil-testing 139
South Downs National Park, decline in grey partridge numbers xiii–xiv, xxi–xxvi
South Downs Way 8, 130, 141-3

Index

Southern Water 72, 121
sparrowhawks 14, 24, 40, 45, 81, 96, 99
stakeholder support, biodiversity projects 33
  see also community outreach work
stewardship schemes 32, 47–8, 66, 72, 74, 139
stoats, control of 79, 84, 85
Stringer, Andrew 16, 19–21, 31–2, 38–9, 46, 52, 58, 84
Stringer, Heather 20
strip cover, hedgerows 18–19
stubble-counts of grey partridges xx–xxi, 50, 57, 123–4, 144, 165
subsidies, agricultural 7, 8
'Sussex Project' xxi
Sussex Study 9, 10, 90, 123–4, 133

thermal-imaging devices 86, 124, 166
'three-legged stool' model 12, 13–25, 34, 49
trees 30, 96, 120
'trophic cascade' 78, 113, 114
Tully trap P6
tunnel traps 83, 85, 87
'turning' the bird, partridge shooting 52
turnips 65, 69, 150

turtle doves 92, 99

Ukraine x, 74, 170

Walker, Kevin 44
walkers 33, 48, 153
War Agricultural Executive Committees 7
water resources 120–1
water utility company 72, 121
weasels 24, 81
  control of 79, 85
weather conditions 68, 80, 171
Wentworth Estate 6
wheat production 7, 31, 65, 74
Whitney, Beau 52, 58
wild pheasants 24, 51, 67
wild plants
  arable flora surveys 92–3, 172
  in conservation headlands 22
  increase in species number 41
Winter, Nigel 105
wolves 77, 78, 114
woodpeckers 96
woodpigeons 40, 96
worms, in soil 65
'wryneck', birds 107

yellowhammers xvii, 26, 87, 133
Yellowstone National Park 77–8

195